*Shakespeare's
Young Lovers*

Dead shepherd, now I find thy saw of might,
' Who ever loved that loved not at first sight? '
— PHEBE, in *As You Like It*

Let thy song be love. This love will undo us all. O Cupid, Cupid, Cupid!
— HELEN, in *Troilus and Cressida*

. . . But these are all lies. Men have died from time to time and worms have eaten them, but not for love.
— ROSALIND

SHAKESPEARE'S YOUNG LOVERS

*The Alexander Lectures
at the University of Toronto*, 1935

BY ELMER EDGAR STOLL

OXFORD UNIVERSITY PRESS
London New York Toronto
1937

Copyright, 1937, by Oxford University Press, New York, Inc.

Printed in the United States of America

Prefatory Note

THESE *lectures have been somewhat changed since delivery and, obviously, enlarged. I wish to express my gratitude to the Macmillan Company and the Cambridge University Press for permission to make use of some ideas in my* SHAKESPEARE STUDIES (1927) *and in my* ART AND ARTIFICE IN SHAKESPEARE (1933); *and to Messrs. Harcourt, Brace and Company for permission to quote a few lines from Mr. Murry's* SHAKESPEARE (1936).

It remains only to express my pleasure in the hospitality and responsiveness of both faculty and students at Toronto; above all in that of the scholar and teacher in whose honour the lectureship was founded. Well for an institution and for a country where learning, critical sanity, and personal qualities like his are so justly recognised!

E.E.S.

Contents

LECTURE I. ROMEO AND JULIET   1

LECTURE II. THE MAIDENS OF
   SHAKESPEARE'S PRIME   45

LECTURE III. THE MAIDENS IN THE
   DRAMATIC ROMANCES   85

SHAKESPEARE'S
YOUNG LOVERS

LECTURE I

Romeo and Juliet

I

FOR these Alexander lectures, which the University of Toronto has done me the honour of inviting me to deliver, I have chosen the subject of Shakespeare's Lovers because (strange as that may sound) of its practical advantages. In a spoken discourse character is easier to handle than structure or style. To be sure, a character is only part of the structure, one member of a group, a constituent element of the action, and no more detachable than a figure in a painting. Of Shakespeare's lovers, however, this is true in a lesser degree than of those of many other dramatists. The late Professor Herford dwelt with pleasure upon their healthiness and normality; the late Professor Frye has insisted that they are even too natural, and 'neither Desdemona, Ophelia, nor Juliet are legitimately heroines of tragedy at all — they are wives and sweethearts who ought to be happily mated and wedded'; and these fine critics are, I think, not really at variance. Most of Shakespeare's lovers in tragedy could with propriety and without much change have been put into comedies, or at least into the romantic sort that Shakespeare nearly always wrote; and those in comedy could have been put into his tragedies. It is not so with Corneille or Racine, Jonson or Molière. In their comedies lovers betray some foible or affectation; in their tragedies, either a fault or a maladjustment. By those dramatists love is dramatized.

By Shakespeare, strictly speaking, it is not. The lovers are less closely implicated with the action, less complicated in themselves. The passion, or the soul that experiences it, is little analysed but is exhibited directly and as a whole; and still less than Shakespeare's other heroes and heroines are the lovers the authors of their own fortune or misfortune. The obstacles to their happiness are not internal, but are villains or enemies, relatives or rivals; they suffer from no inner maladjustments or misunderstandings, but only from those arising out of deception or slander, feigning or disguise. Their jealousy, when they have any — the heroines have none — is ordinarily not born in their bosoms, but injected into them, witness Othello, the Claudio of *Much Ado*, and Posthumus; and as Mr. Middleton Murry has said of the love of Othello and Desdemona, theirs is in itself unclouded. They are too naïve, too sound and open-hearted, to get into a serious inner complication. Their coquetry is open and innocent, as Portia's is when she gives Bassanio reasons for delaying his choice; not deceitful or cruel, as Rosalind's is not when she peeps a little from under the veil of her disguise: it has the attraction, not of sophistication but of unsophistication, or if of coquetry, that which renounces itself, on Juliet's principle,

> Or if thou think'st I am too quickly won,
> I'll frown and be perverse and say thee nay, —
> So thou wilt woo; but else, not for the world.

The only real coquette is Cressida, for Cleopatra is in love and has recourse to coquetry only as a lure. Shakespeare's comedy and tragedy alike are not studies, not human documents; and the passion, arising at first sight, is a simple reaction, to the woman's beauty or the man's noble mien. It is an affair of the imagination, not of the intellect, and, apparently, neither the result of a community of tastes or aspirations, on the one hand, nor the cause of a new envisagement of life or adjustment to it, on the other. In this respect, consequently, the plays are scarcely dramas. The passion is not pitted against others such as ambition or revenge; not brought into conflict with ideals such as honour, or with duties such as those to parents or society. It is generally both spontaneous and contagious, untroubled by fear or doubt or questioning. In short, it is, as Professor Herford finds it, in a state of health and equilibrium, and that does not lend itself to drama; it is in a state of health and happiness to the point of charm and beauty, and that does lend itself to poetry.

2

Now all this is true of Romeo and Juliet, though being, unlike the other lovers with whom we are to deal, in a tragedy, they are in the external action more deeply involved. They fall in love at sight and for ever, and, in their own personal relations, are material only for poetry, not for psychology but for character-drawing. Their struggle is not with each other, nor within themselves, but only with their quarrelling families, against the stars. They do not misunderstand or deceive, allure or elude, suspect or tantalize, turn, naturally or unnaturally, from love to hatred or wreak themselves upon each other, as both in drama and in life lovers not uncommonly do; nor are they swayed or inwardly troubled by their inheritance of enmity, or by filial fealty, or for more than a moment by thoughts of a Capulet's blood on Romeo's hand. There is not even the veil of a disguise between them; and the family prejudices or obligations which for Corneille or Racine would, as in the *Cid*, have been the making of the drama, the dramatist recognizes but avoids. Or is it the lovers themselves that fatefully avoid them, ignore them? 'All for Love and The World Well Lost' might be the title, though in a different sense from Dryden's; and it is not their self-centred absorption and infatuation or any other internal entanglement that brings them to their death, but (the poet makes clear) the feud and destiny.

There is no tragic fault, or (as we shall see) none in the ordinary sense of the word. Certainly there is none of a social or psychological sort. The play itself, like most of Shakespeare's love stories, is conceived in terms not only of poetry but of romance, of *amor vincit omnia;* and these young and tender things are no more to be judged for disobeying and deceiving their parents than Desdemona or Imogen, Florizel or Perdita, Ferdinand or Miranda, who also do. They come to ruin not because, as Butcher says, 'in their newfound rapture they act in defiance of all external obligations.' They so act, to be sure, but the observation has point only as registering a distinction between romance and realism; in so far as their recklessness occurs to us it is meant to redound to the lovers' credit. The point of the play — the wonder of the story — is, not how such a love can arise out of hatred and then triumph over it in death, but that it does. I have reverence for Samuel Butcher: the greatest of critics will commit errors in judgment as he struggles, amid our present-day æsthetic confusion, to expound and apply the *katharsis* and the *hamartia* of Aristotle. I have little for theorists like Gervinus, who complains of Juliet's quibbling and prevaricating with her parents, and concealing her purposes, as she goes to confession, under the mask of piety. Just so he and other Hegelians treat Desdemona, in the light of Eternal Justice, which in Shakespeare, as out in the world, cannot fail! If the Heidelberg professor, so widely read in literature, did not appreciate the romantic tradition, with its plenary indulgence of lovers, even from the times of the Greek romances, he ought, as a Teuton at least, to have remembered the source, the *Quelle,* an Italian novel, an English poem, famous in Shakespeare's day.

3

The social or ethical bias, however, now plays less part in the verdict than the psychological. For some critics the lovers, particularly Romeo, are *not* in equilibrium, and hence their fall. Professor Herford, with Mr. Middleton Murry's approval, holds that Shakespeare conceives of love 'as a condition which, so far from inevitably containing the seed of its own disruption, is so naturally strong that it needs the invasion of an alien power [that is, a villain] to be prevented from the bliss of perfect fulfilment.'[1] Gervinus and Kreyssig, before them, hold in Romeo's case the contrary, and remind us of 'young Werther' (by no means so young though) who, for love not thwarted but unrequited, likewise destroys himself. They show no moderation, no temperance! But Werther is by Goethe elaborately analysed, and, in obedience to Lessing's principle, demonstrated to be the cause of his own undoing. Romeo, like most of Shakespeare's heroes, is neither the one nor the other. Not only is there no suggestion that Romeo's passion is morbid, or that he is in himself unmanly; there is also in Shakespeare's dramaturgy generally, as in the ancient, no requirement that a man's death or ruin should proceed from an inner flaw.[2] The motivation of the action, as in *Hamlet, Othello, King Lear,* and *Macbeth,* though not in *Coriolanus,* is more external; what Professor Herford says of love as a condition not carrying the seed of its own disruption but owing this to an alien power, applies, though he himself would not admit it, to other

1 Murry, *Countries of the Mind* (1922), pp. 9, 15, 26.
2 I have discussed the matter in earlier writing, but most fully in my *Shakespeare and Other Masters,* presently to appear, chap. 2, 'Reconciliation in Tragedy.'

passions in Shakespeare; there the presentation of character is poetical rather than psychological and ethical, as in Greek Tragedy, in Homer and Virgil, and these anxious searchings for a tragic sin are out of place. Above all is that true of such a story as this, and in the resistance of these lovers to their fate they are not really succumbing to it. In Mantua, after his banishment, Romeo has not been pining and moping, absence has not been a torment, and before he gets the news of his lady's death he has, throughout the day, been lifted above the ground with cheerful thoughts. His dream has seemed to him of good omen. But when that has by the news been made an ambiguous mockery, he at once cries out,

> Is it even so? Then I defy you, stars,

in the same spirit as when he looked at the body of Tybalt, whose cousin he had just married, and whose blood, for that reason, he had a moment before refused to shed. 'O, I am fortune's fool!' And such he is now — though not altogether — a second time. Before that, on the point of marriage, he had cried,

> Then, love-devouring Death do what he dare,
> It is enough I may but call her mine.

For in those days men really believed in fortune, in the stars, in Death with his pestilent scythe; and they did so all the more of course when in a tragedy.

That is not the language of weakness, though also not of reason and restraint: It is the lovers' youth that

7

we must bear in memory, and their innocence, for both are heightened and emphasized; and we must equally bear in mind that the play is a poem. Juliet is fourteen, not sixteen as in the source, and Romeo is little more than a lad. In the poet's hands both are far less sophisticated and artful; and a contrast or opposition is kept before us (though always concretely) not only between love and hatred, youth and age (as Mr. Erskine notices) but also between love and death. The struggle is only external, and the drama now and then verges upon the lyric: by Schlegel, Mézières, Professor Herford, and Mr. Murry alike it is called, not the tragedy of love, but love's triumphal hymn; and not because there is anything wrong with them do the youth and maiden perish but only because 'love is strong as death,' and fate unfriendly. At the end, when the feud is allayed, the families reconciled, ' the spring and the winter meet,' says Coleridge, the poet, 'winter assumes the character of spring, and spring the sadness of winter.' At the end I myself always think of Watts' two paintings *Love and Death* and *Love Triumphant;* and drama is here reduced to the simplicity of poetry.

4

As a youth Romeo enjoys immunities; and one of these, at the outset, is that of being 'love-bewildered,' as Coleridge puts it, in love with love in the distant and cruel shape of Rosaline. To this he proves his right, for once he sets eyes upon Juliet he is in love indeed and is himself again. The lovesickness, evidently, was transitory and normal. It is now in a different vein that he talks, not only to Juliet but (of every-day matters) to other people. He can jest again — lovesick lovers cannot — and more than hold his own at the game against Mercutio. And thereupon that expert at the sport is delighted. 'Why, is not this better,' he cries, ' than groaning for love? Now art thou sociable, now art thou Romeo, now art thou what thou art, by art as well as by Nature.' No longer does he pace under the sycamores by night or pen sonnets in a dark room by day. Here may seem to be an instance of a resultant adjustment to life such as I have to Shakespeare's lovers just denied; but it is rather a readjustment; and in any case it is not explained. ' The English mind,' says Mr. Basil de Selincourt, ' has a native affinity for unanalysed adjustments and reactions '; and Shakespeare's mind, of course, is eminently English. All there is to the present situation is that the youth had been healthy and lively enough before the recent perturbation, as appears not only from Mercutio's words but from the previous anxious comments of his parents, and now by a real and solid love has been restored. He is no sentimentalist or philanderer. And surely it is no weakling or Werther that avenges Mercutio or, still less, that, rising above the requirements of the punctilio, spares Tybalt when he challenges him before this. These high external obligations he unmistakably and gloriously heeds.

Dowden, who has admirably refuted the critics'

dour morality, particularly that of Gervinus, is still troubled by their psychology. He does remember Romeo's youth but seems not fully to appreciate the naturalness and temporariness of his lovesickness. He compares him with Hamlet, and thinks his will is sapped, though by a different disease of soul. 'To him . . . emotion, apart from thought and apart from action, is an end in itself.' His is a serious condition, and while he is eventually cured by his real love for Juliet, he is not at once. No doubt Dowden is affected by the greater imaginativeness of Romeo's wooing than of Juliet's and by his lamentations in the Friar's cell. To both we shall recur.

If Romeo be morbid, Juliet, who dies to join him, even as he has died to join her, must surely be the same; but of that, naturally enough, little has been said. If Juliet cannot pass the censor, who, pray, can? Another charge, made by both the Germans and also the Swedes — but not, happily, by such as Schlegel, Brandes, Brandl, and Creizenach — is that these Italian passions are unbalanced in another meaning of the word, that is, sensual; and here Juliet, in her frank and eager expectation of her wedding-night, bears the burden of reproach, though in so far as lack of acquaintance at the outset is also matter for deprecation, Romeo shares it. 'So much I say with confidence,' declares Henrik Schück, quoted by Brandes; 'that the woman who, inaccessible to the spiritual element in love, lets herself be carried away on this first meeting by the joy of the senses . . . that woman is ignorant of the love which our age demands.' That age, I hasten however to remind you, is now two generations old!

5

I have not read this scholar or Hartmann, who shares with him the credit of the grim opinion, to discover whether this impetuosity in welcoming love is, like the lovers' impetuosity in seeking death when deprived of it, taken for a tragic fault, the cause of the catastrophe; but by writers so ethical and judicial we may well suppose it to be. Again one wonders at the critics' failure to remember early literature, particularly the romantic. In medieval and Renaissance story, whether verse or prose, epic, ballad, or drama, it is love at first sight generally, without regard to reason or prudence. Was Dante sensual? But it was so that he fell in love in the *Vita Nuova*, and how many words had he had with the maiden before she died? What, moreover, do these critics make of Shakespeare elsewhere? Are Rosalind, Viola, Olivia, Miranda, and their lovers, too, no better than they should be, no more respectable and continent, indeed, than the actors and actresses that ordinarily undertake to play them? As at least romantic poets know, extremes may meet, outwardly high romance is not far removed from folly, and Coleridge's ethereal Genevieve falls into her cavalier's arms without waiting for a proposal. To the casual onlooker, Romeo and Juliet may seem to love and marry as carelessly and unthinkingly as folk do at Hollywood or at college; but not to us, who know them. 'The love which is the best ground of marriage,' says who but the saintly and also 'judicious' Hooker, author of the *Laws of Ecclesiastical Polity*, in 1584, 'is that which is least able to render a reason for itself.'

In drama, at any rate, if not in life, there is justification enough for this instantaneous and explosive temperament — in drama, which has no more than three or four hours at its disposal, above all the Elizabethan, which tells the whole story, not, like the modern, merely the last chapter, and, whether in tragedy or in comedy, often more stories than one. And what is as important, stories with action, incidents, and vicissitudes; the taste of the Elizabethan theatrical public, and (so far as we know) that of its most popular purveyor, not easily contenting itself, like Drinkwater's and Guitry's, without plot or complication. Hence the need of the dramatist's availing himself of summary and compendious devices; and this of love at first sight, in *Romeo and Juliet, As You Like It*, the *Tempest*, in *Twelfth Night* thrice over, in *Much Ado* so far as Claudio is concerned, ties the knot of the complication and precipitates the action like another, that of slander, in *Othello, Much Ado, Cymbeline*, the underplot of *King Lear*. Both devices, like overhearing and soliloquy, disguise and mistaken identity, are short cuts, contrivances to that end highly desirable in drama — compression and intensity. Time in *Romeo and Juliet*, as in most of Shakespeare's love stories when compared with their sources, has been reduced by the dramatist from a stretch of months to one of days, in this to four — there, if nowhere else, are the trammels of psychology and realism flung aside! And if Romeo and Juliet, in a story which is also that of a feud and the Capulets' match-making, had been required to proceed properly and decorously through the psychologically and socially appropriate stages of acquaintance and a growing attachment, Juliet, indeed, would, like most flesh-and-blood Italian girls of her era, have been fast married to Paris before ever her heart had awakened. In the play as it is, compression permits of comprehension. Through the instantaneousness of the love-making, there are, on the same principle, both room and warrant for an in itself improbable number of external events and an in itself improbable range of internal development. In their three days the inexperienced pair grow up before us, to tragic stature. Juliet breaks away from the counsellor of her childhood and dares to take the potion, Romeo because of his love puts up with insults from Tybalt, despite his love avenges Mercutio, and either of them unhesitatingly has recourse to death in order to rejoin the other. And these doings are made plausible, not of course by analysis or adequate motivation, but as we shall see, by the temper and utterance of the youth or the maiden, which harden and deepen without losing their identity.

The merely dramatic conventions and requirements, however, are here less significant than the narrative, which are older. Conventions, which, when they are telling and effective, are, as Mr. Lucas says, born, not made, are still more telling and effective (until they are threadbare) if they have been born long before. Such conventions as our impressionism and cubism in painting or literature were certainly made, and within a generation; but love at first sight began with the story of Adam and Eve, and the calumniator credited (very probably) even before Joseph and Potiphar, Bellerophon and Proetus. That in this particular story the romantic effect of such an emotional explosion, though on the stage naturally greater, had already proved striking, appears from the many versions before Shakespeare approached the subject. Even reading the *novella* or poem, the public had delighted in this angelical cry of love arising, unexpectedly and spontaneously, from out of the harsh tumult of quarrel, in defiance of death.

Moreover, the thing has actually happened, to folk quite above the cultural level of our first parents in the garden; this convention is not remote from reality: and in the case before us the only question should be whether it is made plausible. There is motivation, of a sort; yet here again there is little analysis and still less of novelty, but the summary method followed in Shakespeare's other love stories, and if this one does not satisfy Teutonic and Scandinavian rigour, I do not see how the others can. One of my students, with a German given name and a North-British surname, has, with the acuteness of the latter race and the laboriousness of the former, examined and tabulated the data in Shakespeare generally; and these turn out to be surprisingly like those in the medieval epic poets and troubadours and the Renaissance sonneteers. As already suggested, and as of such impetuosity could be expected, Shakespeare's heroes love their ladies for their beauty, pure and simple. When they go into detail, it is still a matter mainly of externals. Not the face but the white hand is most fondly dwelt upon, but what *motif* is more ancient? There is the 'lily-white' one of the popular ballads, and its equivalent in Chaucer, the medieval romances, Catullus, Propertius, Ovid, and even Theocritus. After the hand in importance comes the breath; then the eyes; then the hair, nearly always golden; then the lips of coral and the voice of silver: all traditional enough. Sometimes the form, the carriage, and the gait are touched upon; and once love has its way, qualities and accomplishments, but in terms that might be duplicated everywhere in earlier poetry. Two of the heroines, says Mr. Montgomery, are loved for their 'virtues,' but what these are we do not learn. Seven are praised for their chastity, four because they are 'true.' 'Sweet,' 'gentle,' 'tender,' 'modest,' are the other most frequent attributes; and Silvia is called 'holy,' Imogen 'good.' These adjectives, though not so often repeated, are scarcely more specific than the 'standing epithets' of the ballads and of Homer and Virgil. The accomplishments are more seldom praised and less dilated upon — wit and excellence in discourse, singing, playing, dancing, and skill at needlework. And what the women, for their part, admire in their lovers is beauty too — here again Shakespeare might be found insufficiently Nordic, and regrettably akin to Homer and Virgil, who take time and pains to tell us who were the handsomest warriors — but the ladies are still less original and analytical, though they pay more attention to form and bearing, less to curls and complexion, and for accomplishments and virtues prefer the martial and noble.

6

In short, the reasons for the love are as summary and traditional as the manner of its appearance; and in the play before us it is, again, by the heroine's beauty that the hero is captivated, even as in the medieval troubadours and romancers. At various times he momentarily praises her eyes, hand, cheek, and lips; but has nothing to say of her wit, wisdom, and chastity though he has had something to say of Rosaline's. There is no occasion, for he does not fall into discussion of her with Benvolio; but he might well have done so with the Friar as he informed him of the change, and the omission is only a clearer indication how little precise and fundamental motiving counts. We have seen already how love brings the pair to their death only as in a poem or fable, without psychological causation, and it is so that their love arises. In Shakespeare elsewhere, as in most other Elizabethan drama, love, like jealousy and villainy, is as sudden; and a good deal of the motiving is traditional and superficial, more narrative or epical than strictly dramatic. It is for the story, to get the action started, as in the present instance, or to keep it moving, as in that (later to be considered) of Romeo's and the whole Capulet family's precipitate conduct. It is pretty arbitrary, with little reason or provocation, though there may have been some in the source. So it is with Viola's love in *Twelfth Night*, for in the original she had met the Duke and loved him long since; with Antonio's sadness, in the *Merchant of Venice*, for in the original the Merchant was Bassanio's godfather and was troubled ' on account of his ill-successes ' ; with Leontes' jealousy, for in the original it develops gradually and has some cause and occasion; with Iago's and Don John's slanders, for in the original both men were rejected and embittered suitors; with Hamlet's feigned madness, for in Belleforest the murderer was known and the madness was a safeguard; with Macbeth's regicide, for in Holinshed the thane was not the king's host, and had besides a grievance against him, a claim to the throne. Often, too, what reasons are given by the dramatist are inadequate, or the motive itself is out of all proportion or relation to the injury; and Mr. Bradley himself notices that the Ancient takes little pleasure in Cassio's place once he is possessed of it, nor does he comport himself like a jealous husband, getting even wife for wife. So with less momentous matters, in comedy, as when Olivia will not listen to a wooer because of her mourning for her brother, but soon quite forgets her grief, even as the twins Viola and Sebastian do theirs for the loss of each other; and as when Rosalind and Celia go to the forest to meet their father and uncle but don't trouble much about him once they arrive. What in all these cases is secured, is motivation not for psychology but for story; and having, like Lear's irascibility and Macbeth's ambition, served its purpose at the beginning of the play, it is dropped.[3] For by then the passions, the objective of every true dramatist, ancient or modern, are in full career.

7

What interests Shakespeare, and should interest us, is not so much the motives but what is moved; that is, the action, of which the characters are a part but not the source; the poem, which is not a study of the passions, but a presentation of a contrast or conflict between them and of the harmony in their effect upon us, and not much of any conflict within the single bosom, either, as it is with Corneille and Racine. For Romeo and Juliet the path is pretty straight and undeviating, still more so than for Othello, Lear, Hamlet, and Macbeth; all that the young man has to contend with is the hatred of the families, and the stars, which lend the feud the dignity of a fate. In the tragedy the quarrel plays a larger part than in the source; it is the fate-*motif*, and four times, at critical moments, it makes itself audible and visible — at the ball and at the deaths of the Prince's kinsman, of Mercutio and Tybalt, of

3 For Macbeth cf. J. W. Mackail, *Approach to Shakespeare*, p. 106.

Paris and the lovers — as the Ghost in *Hamlet* and the Weird Sisters in *Macbeth* do thrice. And to the ominous luminaries above Romeo lifts his eyes before he enters the ball-room, when he hears the news of Juliet's death, and before he dies himself. It is a simple and sensuous, imaginative and passionate effect at which the poet is aiming.

Romeo's love for Rosaline has long been taken to be an internal preparation; it is — for an external contrast and surprise. No doubt there is a psychological reality in the passing of a hopeless lovesickness, under the spell of a higher influence, into love itself; but there is none in its doing this so completely and instantaneously, as the youth comes to the dance to see Rosaline, not, as in the source, to find a substitute for his obdurate mistress, but to prove her more beautiful than any. The contrast is external; there is no struggle or hesitation; to Rosaline, from now on, he gives not another thought. Instead of natural and psychological, gradual and probable, Romeo's falling in love is made the contrary; and this simply to produce the greater effect for Juliet's beauty and for the love that, without consideration of family, rank, or any other terrestrial concern, takes possession of both. The Rosaline affair has, further, the purely dramatic or poetic advantage of offering an interesting contrast between Romeo's demeanour now and before, and (with comic effect) between the past and the present connection, as Mercutio thinks him still in love with Rosaline or else no longer in love at all, or as the Friar, fearing the sleepless youth has passed the night with her, learns he would now be married to another:

> Holy Saint Francis, what a change is here!

'Just what I expected,' he might have said, and either he or somebody else in the play should have said, if the psychological theory were sound.

It is a surprise for him, who does not and could not know the lovers and their feelings as we do; but, though of a different sort, it was meant to be a surprise for us in the first place. It is poetically, dramatically, not psychologically, that the characters are meant to interest us, even more than in Shakespeare generally; and as usually in Shakespeare's tragedy and even in comedy (witness Benedick and Beatrice), they do this more deeply because they are in a situation not wholly of their making. In the case just mentioned there is no surprise: the two wranglers fall in love as a result of a deception. But while their scoffing at love and gibing at each other may be taken to be signs of their interest in both, there is no psychical verisimilitude to either their credulity or their sudden change. It is for the contrast, the emotional and comic effect. In the case before us, however, the comic effect is subordinate and incidental, arising in connection with Romeo alone; the emotional is all-absorbing. It is contrary to psychology, contrary to nature, that in the presence of Juliet the romantic Romeo should forget Rosaline at once and for good and all; but that he should do so throws his love for Juliet into high relief.

The great emotional situation is what Shakespeare was seeking; and in this early and lesser tragedy Romeo is swept off his feet by love as, in the later ones, Othello, Posthumus, and Leontes are by jealousy, Macbeth by ambition, Hamlet by the Ghost's revelations and command, and Lear by thwarted paternal affection. And for the full impression we need — we must have — no analysis or previously indicated inclination, but a Romeo thinking, the moment before, of another woman when we hear him break out at the ball, at the sight of Juliet:

O, she doth teach the torches to burn bright!

and we need a Juliet who has already averred that matrimony is an honour that she dreams not of, when she bids her Nurse

Go ask his name. — If he be marrièd,
My grave is like to be my wedding-bed . . .

a Juliet and a Romeo each aware, the moment after, that the other is an enemy. For the full impression, moreover, we need the traditional, the simple and sensuous motive of the maiden's beauty. With the full force of the impression a more spiritual motive, even could it here be adequately provided, would interfere.

And the emotional situation is justified or made acceptable, as often in Shakespeare, not by analysis and realism, but by stage management, by poetry, by the fitness of the situation in the world that the poet has created. Instead of a definite psychological transition from Rosaline to Juliet, there is, for plausibility's sake, a slight interval after Romeo's outcry (which the hero may be supposed to use for reflection and readjustment) bridged by the quarrel between the testy Tybalt and the hospitable Capulet; and instead of the long and tedious process of getting acquainted and making love, there is a wooing which is lifted above the level of life by rime and brought within the compass of a sonnet. This way of courting and mating is appropriate in Shakespeare's romantic Verona, as Othello's sudden jealousy is in a Venice and a Cyprus where Iago enjoys such a reputation, or Imogen's crediting Iachimo after Posthumus has, by his letter of introduction, done the same.[4] That the youth and the maiden should fall in love at sight is not out of keeping with their at once making the fact known to each other, with her doing more than the girl's ordinary share of the wooing and his forgetting Rosaline on the spot; with the thought of both that this is a matter of union or of death, in disregard of all prudential or practical considerations, in defiance of the stars; and with their high poetical ways of talking generally as well as the romantic incidents and setting — masques, balls, tempestuous quarrels and duels, endearments in the moonlight and bidding adieu at dawn, a wedding in a Friar's cell and a ladder to reach the wedding-bed, and thereupon the sleeping-potion, the burial alive to escape the accepted suitor, the reunion only in the grave. It is a thoroughly romantic world (though a more turbulent

4 Cf. below, p. 96.

and passionate one), as in the *Midsummer Night's Dream, The Merchant of Venice, As You Like It, Twelfth Night*, and nearly all the rest, where more or less similarly the premature falling in love is made plausible.

Furthermore, the motive for it, the maiden's beauty, is made adequate and convincing by its retention — the maiden's attraction is the wife's — and its retention is owing to its poetic and dramatic advantages. In the tomb scene it is still Juliet's 'beauty' that moves the hero, making the vault a lantern, 'a feasting presence full of light.' Upon that death 'hath had no power,' its 'ensign yet is crimson in thy lips and in thy cheeks, and death's pale flag is not advancèd there.' 'Thou art not conquer'd,' in his immortal words. A more soberly edifying and satisfying spectacle might have been made out of his considering Juliet's spiritual qualities; her soul it might have been that is not conquered; but Romeo is like Othello, yet to come. In that tragedy the motivation, at the outset, is less traditional, though as summarily romantic:

> She lov'd me for the dangers I had pass'd,
> And I lov'd her that she did pity them.

But presently for him too the woman's charm is her beauty; and it is by this sensuous simplification that his love for her is kept before us in the midst of his jealous anguish: — 'the fair devil'; 'lest her body and beauty unprovide my mind again'; 'lest being like one of heaven the devils themselves should fear to seize thee';

'Oh, thou weed, who art so lovely fair and smell'st so sweet, that the sense aches at thee.' Better this than any exposition.

8

The method, then, is imaginative and immediate, impulsive and emotional, dramatic or at least structural and poetic, not (happily) psychological or sociological. The motives, in so far as there are any — Juliet's beauty and her particular features — are dwelt upon but to start the story and support the situation; and that the lovers are fitted for each other appears indirectly and incidentally — they themselves are not concerned about it — as with Benedick and Beatrice, Orlando and Rosalind, Florizel and Perdita, Ferdinand and Miranda. If not otherwise, by their fruits we know them, — health out of lovesickness, daring and resourcefulness out of inexperience. But the chief thing is that we should be made to feel the greatness of their love and then in each of them find warrant for it. If Othello is called noble, Desdemona gentle, and Iago (in his villainous hypocrisy) 'honest', we must, in order to yield the author full credence, be convinced of it in our own right. So we must be impressed directly by Romeo's and Juliet's reality and charm; for ourselves we must be led to acknowledge that each is worth the winning; and in this play, as in the other and in Shakespeare generally, that is done, again, not by analysis, but by poetry and the quality and individuality of their speech.

To be sure, they are characterized by their deeds as

well (where these are not determined by the requirements of the plot) and by their sentiments. Both lovers are poetical and imaginative; but Romeo is more a prey to his imagination and is less compact and practical, less ready and resolute, as young men commonly are. It is Juliet that first thinks of matrimony and the means to secure it, whether in the ballroom or on the balcony. It is she that arranges for wedding, priest, and means of communication, while Romeo is still rapt and lost in love's young dream. (No wonder, after passing from out of one dream into another!) When marriage to Paris is threatened she welcomes any escape, by knife or poison or a slumber in a tomb; when, at the end, she wakens from it, her words are few, her deed unhesitating. And like a girl or woman, she lives more in her affections and prejudices, is more personal and concrete. She is far more troubled at finding Romeo to be a Montague than he is at finding her to be a Capulet; her grief at the killing of Tybalt, though genuine, is at once overwhelmed by resentment against the Nurse for abusing her lover. Only a new feeling can subdue the old. Twice she curses the Nurse, both now and when she is advised to give up Romeo for Paris. 'Ancient damnation' is equivalent to 'damned old woman,' though not so vulgar; and that is not the only time that her language is passionately but appropriately improper. Yet, true to her sex, she is both more explosive than Romeo and, when need be, more self-contained. On the second occasion she keeps her anger to herself until the Nurse has left the room, just as she presently does her true feelings and purposes from her father and mother. And it is the same concreteness in her frank and ardent expectation of her wedding-night. Sanctioned by the highly moral Coleridge and Hazlitt, this surely need not be defended today; even at this seat and refuge of classical learning people read, I dare say with some measure of approval, not many, I hope, but the best of contemporary novels, and those who don't, why, they may go back to their Catullus, Tibullus, and Propertius, to Theocritus and the Anthology. Here, needless to say, is nothing like the frankness there; and if purity is a matter of balance, of equipoise and sanity, of the ideal to match and animate the real, then certainly in Juliet we have it, who thinks of Romeo not only as a man but as a kindred spirit, and who, before she knows of him, answering her mother on the subject of matrimony, speaks from out of the rare upper region of romance:

> It is an honour that I dream not of.

She is not in love with love, as Romeo has been; nearly three centuries later, Charlotte Brontë, in *Jane Eyre*, gave offence to her readers by presenting her heroine in that state, permissible enough for the hero; and if Shakespeare had attempted the like, how he would have put her at the mercy of the philosophical Teutons! This virginal innocence of hers is thrown into high relief by the Nurse's chipping in—

> An honour! were not I thine only nurse,
> I would say thou hadst sucked wisdom from thy teat;

much as her conjugal devotion is two days later — time and life move swiftly here — by the Nurse's counsel to give up Romeo and marry again. All in all she is evidently a jewel worth the winning; and in poetry, at any rate, would not be more so if, instead of surrendering to love at discretion, she had deliberately and circumspectly considered whether the youth possessed the solid and substantial qualities desirable in a husband and father.

9

It is mainly, however, in their speech or methods of expression that the finer discrimination of their characters and the elements of their charm reside. Romeo's imagination flies higher, ranges more widely, and it is he that has the figure of adventure:

> I am no pilot; yet wert thou as far
> As that vast shore wash'd with the farthest sea,
> I should adventure for such merchandise . . .

which he echoes in the tomb scene:

> Thou desperate pilot, now at once run on
> The dashing rocks thy sea-sick weary bark

just as it is he that has visions of glory like this in the tomb:

> Thou art not conquer'd, beauty's ensign yet
> Is crimson in thy lips and in thy cheeks,
> And death's pale flag is not advancèd there,

and this on facing the dawn after the wedding-night:

> Night's candles are burnt out and jocund day
> Stands tiptoe on the misty mountain tops.

In both the later passages there is a fuller and richer melody than in the earlier ones. It is proper that such an experience as his should have left its impress upon him.

Juliet's imagination is simpler, less frankly poetical but more naïve and individual; and it is pervaded with her girlish playfulness, which, except in anger, seldom deserts her. As in her wooing, for of that she does her share:

> 'Tis almost morning, I would have thee gone; —
> And yet no farther than a wanton's bird;
> That lets it hop a little from her hand,
> Like a poor prisoner in his twisted gyves,
> And with a silken thréad plúcks it báck agáin . . .

(There she plucks it!) And even in meditating up amid the constellations:

> Come, gentle night, come, loving, black-brow'd night,
> Give me my Romeo; and when he shall die,
> Take him and cut him out in little stars,
> And he will make the face of heaven so fine
> That all the world will be in love with night,
> And pay no worship to the garish sun . . .

Both make love wittily and humorously, as most of Shakespeare's young people do; but Juliet's playful or caressing, confiding or cajoling manner is something that is more native and inseparable, as when she coaxes the Nurse to tell her the news,

> Sweet, sweet, sweet nurse, tell me, what says my love?

or when she takes refuge with her for comfort:

> Cómfort me, cóunsel me

. . . . .

> What sáy'st thou? Hast thou not a wórd of jóy?
> Sòme cómfort, núrse?

With Angelica she is a child, and still more than most charming women she is something of a child with her lover. ' I would I were thy bird,' whispers Romeo:

> Sweet, so would I;
> Yet I should kill thee with much cherishing.

The great effect, however, the perfect, unexpected touch, upon which I have twice elsewhere commented but am all the more eager to do so again, is as she wakes to find the cup in his hand. ' O churl,' she murmurs, — ' bad boy ' —

> O churl! drunk all, and left no friendly drop
> To help me after!

To him she speaks, not of him. He is only a step away, in a moment she herself will take it, and on his heedlessness she rallies him. Whether this is imagination in her or a childish want of it, there is no doubt what it is in the poet himself as he now sees her lips lifting at the corners as of old.

Though kept identical, however, the pair, as I have already intimated, develop, too rapidly for realism but not for poetry. ' Go, counsellor,' she mutters after the Nurse has advised compliance:

> Thou and my bosom henceforth shall be twain.

Give me, she bids the Friar when he proposes the dangerous potion,

> Gíve me, gíve me! O, tell not me of féar!

she, who a few moments before had been begging for comfort. But the greater change is in Romeo, from lovesickness back to his lively witty self that we have not yet known, but Mercutio has and delights in, then to the self-restraint under Tybalt's insults, then to the manly retaliation for Mercutio's death, then to the calm of a desperate resolve as he receives the news:

> Is it even so? Then I defy you, stars.

> Well, Juliet, I will lie with thee to-night.

He is a man now, not a lad; there is now no wailing or ranting as in the Friar's cell. And in the changes of mood and tone that follow there is no more of the extravagance or egotism of passion. He can think of others — considers the misery of the apothecary and wonders at him:

> Art thou so base and full of wretchedness
> And fear'st to die?

and, paying him, bids him 'buy food and get thyself in flesh.' As before the tomb he tells Balthasar to be gone, he adds,

> Live, and be prosperous; and farewell, good fellow;

and Paris, who interposes, he beseeches,

> Good gentle youth, tempt not a desperate man.

Though Paris is as yet unknown to him, when he falls, begging to be laid with Juliet, Romeo answers at once, ' In faith, I will,' and then recognizing him, in an outburst of generosity:

> What said my man, when my betossed soul
> Did not attend him as we rode? I think
> He told me Paris should have married Juliet.
> Said he not so? Or did I dream it so?
> Or am I mad, hearing him talk of Juliet,
> To think it was so? O, give me thy hand,
> One writ with me in sour misfortune's book!
> I'll bury thee in a triumphant grave. . .

So in the tomb, at the sight of Tybalt in his bloody sheet, he cries,

> Forgive me, cousin!

He is even so grown up and self-forgetful in his passion as to let his wits have play, or, as he expresses it, be a little 'merry.' When at the purchase of the poison, the Apothecary excuses himself —

> My poverty, not my will, consents,

he catches him up and helps him through the loophole —

I pay thy poverty, and not thy will;

and now, even as he drinks, he remembers him and his assurances —

                O true apothecary!
Thy drugs are quick.

A man, he has at the supreme moment, more thoughts than a single one, like Raleigh, Sir Thomas More, the Emperor Vespasian, and like Hamlet, who, under the shadow of death, bandies words with the Gravedigger and Osric. He is not a Werther, though at the outset he bade fair to be.

10

Only once does he or Juliet speak out of character, sing off key. It is, of course, where she receives the news of Tybalt's death and where Romeo in the Friar's cell laments its consequences. Both rant, though in different fashion. Juliet, in her excitement and resentment, takes to quibbles and conceits, to oxymorons such as 'fiend angelical,' to both verbal and logical antics; and Romeo, as Mr. Granville-Barker puts it, breaks into hysterics, metaphorically, that is to say. This is, no doubt, in some measure to be attributed to the immaturity of Shakespeare's art, for the play is an early one. But why these false notes in connexion with the chief characters and not the others? With them, except amid the hubbub of the family's lamentation over Juliet's apparent death — and even there the Nurse at least is recognizable — the dramatist's hand scarcely swerves. How vividly and truly Mercutio, the merry man, subsides into the 'grave man,' still punning, in spirit by Tybalt's deadly thrust not killed! It is not merely a matter of immaturity but, relatively, a fairly permanent feature of Shakespeare's genius and even of the dramatic art. In most dramas, as in many great novels, the minor characters are more continuously and unmistakably identical because, not being at the centre and vortex of the action, they do not undergo the strain or experience the changes that the principal characters do. And this is true of Shakespeare in an especial degree. His tragedy being, like the ancient, a system and harmony of passions, and those in their extremity and violence,[5] the principal personages must fairly run the gamut of them, passing from happiness to grief, from calm or indifference to rage or despair. In the process, the outlines of common humanity are not infrequently troubled or obscured, whether the writing be good or, as in the present instance, faulty. So it is now and then with Lear in the extremity of his indignation against his daughters, and with Hamlet, as when on jumping into the grave he mouths and rants against Ophelia's brother. When passion is treated and developed thus freely and poetically, in the form of imprecation or invective, exclamation or apostrophe, reproach or lamentation, full-throated rage or despair, which have

[5] See the essay on 'The Dramatic Texture,' *Criterion*, July 1935.

only a limited relation to the language of ordinary life, it cannot always be perfectly fitted to the character and the occasion. Romeo now must have a grief adequate to his misfortune, and commensurate with his former happiness; indeed, in his extravagance at this point in the story, he is but following the Romeo of the source. The hero's lack of reticence and reserve, moreover, which equals his lack of restraint in action, is partly owing to the same frank and open, not only lyrical but self-descriptive method, whether passion is or is not thus given the rein. The sadness of Antonio, the melancholy of Jaques, the wearing of their hearts upon their sleeves by nearly all the male lovers in Shakespeare — Romeo, Orsino, Claudio, Bassanio, Orlando — are not the weakness of the sex. The males, as the more active dramatic agents, have only more need or occasion.

Something similar, however, may be said of Juliet, who, unlike most of Shakespeare's tragic heroines, stands, on hearing of Tybalt's death, in the foreground. Her character then shows up more clearly than her lover's, as when, roused by the Nurse's partisan execration, ' Shame come to Romeo,' she breaks out,

> Blister'd be thy tongue
> For such a wish! he was not born to shame . .

but in general the writing of the scene is as bad, and in one matter, the effort to present a contention of emotions, a heart divided against itself, Shakespeare betrays an inability that he was never to overcome. His dialectic is not equal to the passions he arouses. How different the effect of these oxymorons and paradoxes, these whys and wherefores of the killing and of her own weeping, and this weighing the banishment of her lover in the balance against the death of all her kin, from the truly passionate antitheses of Corneille's Chimène as she considers her lover's slaying of her father, and resolves

> Le poursuivre, le perdre, et mourir après lui.

Juliet is as formal and superficial as Richard III after seeing the ghosts,

> What! do I fear myself? There's none else by.
> Richard loves Richard: that is, I am I . . .

and is almost as intellectually and ethically confused as Brutus when he takes account beforehand of his reasons for killing Cæsar. (Why Shakespeare's Brutus did it no one will ever know.) With her the tragic struggle is only skin-deep, and once the Nurse chimes in, it is over; whereas Chimène loves Rodrigue, for defending his own and his father's honour, all the more, and even to be *worthy* of him seeks vengeance upon him for her father's death:

> Je me dois, par ta mort, montrer digne de toi.

For such passionate and dramatic debate, internal and external, Shakespeare had in his theatre no model — in his public, perhaps, no taste and in himself little talent

— and often later, as when Antony forsakes Cleopatra for Octavia and then the latter for the former, he deliberately avoids it. He has other methods to indicate the transition; and it is not in analysis that lay his power but in synthesis, not in a clash but in a contrast, not in the reasoned contention of opposed emotions but in the juxtaposition or merging of them, as when Hamlet bids Ophelia get her to a nunnery and Othello insults Desdemona, when Phoebe both disparages and praises Rosalind-Ganymede and Helen timidly begs Bertram for a kiss. In the present play even of this there is none. After the first shock (as we have seen) Juliet and Romeo alike give no thought to the blood on his hand, just as before this they have given none to their parents' claims or to the marriage arranged with Paris. At the first they but coo and sing to each other like two birds in the garden;[6] and except for the shadow of death upon them they do the same as they part after their wedding-night.

In the heart of the dutiful and revengeful Chimène there is as much love as in Juliet's, but it is more dramatically expressed, breaking through the surface. 'Go away,' she cries, but she means, says Sainte-Beuve, the contrary; and for a moment, but only one, they too dream and sing, like the Capulet and the Montague:

Va-t-en, on sent que cela veut dire: *Reste*. Il reste en effet; tous deux se rapprochent et se mettent à rêver, comme dans *Roméo et Juliette:*

[6] Cf. Granville-Barker, *Prefaces*, Sec. Series, p. 54.

> Que de maux et de pleurs nous coûteront nos pères.

Et ce délicieux retour sur le passé:

> Rodrigue, qui l'eût cru?
>   — Chimène, qui l'eût dit? [7]

Our hero and heroine sing on untroubled.

All for love, and right they are. But if there has so far been no fault, is there not a sign of one in Romeo's hysterics, and some miserable little warrant for Gervinus? Apart from the considerations of technique and source we must remember that this represents only a momentary aberration, Romeo being manly enough before and after. Indeed, there is a kind of superficially psychological propriety in Romeo's hysterics as a fleeting reaction — a relapse, necessary under the stress of circumstances, to the condition he was in at the outset. His youth we should again remember. At that age all for love, like the love of love beforehand, is nearly normal.

11

This applies also to the less unsympathetic psychology of Dowden. At Tybalt's death there is not much to choose between Romeo and Juliet in the extravagance of their grief; and the unfavourable contrast with her does not hold. She indulges her emotions almost as much as he. At other times, as we have seen, he enjoys a wider range of imagination and emotion; but that is proper enough, and characteristic of the sex in life —

---

[7] *Nouveaux lundis* (1872), VII, p. 278.

are not men, instead of women, the poets and artists? — as in Shakespeare generally. But here it is mainly, as it often is in Shakespeare, a matter of poetical rather than psychological continuity and propriety. One who has been indulging his sentiments and fancies before they had a worthy object or occasion will appropriately enough do that still when they have one, without therefore deserving the charge of being sentimental. And wider range of imagination, greater volume of emotion is surely to be expected of one who for the purposes of dramatic effect has undergone such a revulsion as his at the Capulets' ball!

It is not for the hysterics, however, that the moralizing critics most commonly take Romeo to task: he is on the whole quite too vigorous to be morbid. It is for that other impetuosity which we have already touched upon — in marrying, killing, and running to meet death himself. If he had waited, had inquired and coolly considered, and, as Rümelin and others have insisted, if both had made a clean breast of the matter to their parents, they might have lived as man and wife, if not in Verona, in Mantua! (If for nothing else, such remarks serve to make clearer the nature of drama and poetry, the difference between them and psychology and life.) Along with this, ordinarily, is involved a charge against the author's structural art; for what is it but chance that keeps the messenger of the Friar from arriving? Certainly the play would have been more logical and compact if, as one good critic would have it do, 'the same fatality which passes through

Mercutio found its mark at last in hero and heroine,'[8] and thus their deaths were more directly and evidently the result of the quarrel. But for the Elizabethans and their age and, I fancy, for a goodly number of the unsophisticated even today, such a sociological study and demonstration would have been too tame and narrow, would not have offered sufficient emotional and poetic scope. The stars, though they may be taken for the Elizabethan equivalent of our modern 'environment,' 'society,' or 'heredity,' are really another matter. Those fateful orbs appear in the Prologue as presiding. It is of them that Romeo speaks in his foreboding as he goes to the ball; it is they, not human institutions or enmity, that he defies as he hears of her death; and it is their yoke that he shakes from his world-wearied flesh as he expires. This makes for compactness, though of a sort, to be sure, less logical and more external; and how much loftier a flight for the hero's imagination than any conceivable heroic variation upon Mercutio's 'A plague o' both your houses' — 'o' both our houses' — at the end, though the like would make for a more reasoned and solid, a more up-to-date dramaturgy! No doubt the quarrel might fittingly, and to our academic taste more dramatically, be now again at the end the instrument of fate or fortune; but then the malign power of fate or fortune would be less apparent. That effect is

---

[8] Professor Frye, *Romance and Tragedy* (1922), p. 297. Cf. in my article, 'The Tragic Fallacy,' in the *Toronto Quarterly*, July, 1936, or my book cited above, p. 6, the same complaint against a similarly less compact and logical, but more poetic and dramatic, method employed by Ibsen in *Rosmersholm*.

necessary to provoke the hero's defiance; the hero's defiance is necessary to motive his headlong rush to death; his headlong rush to death, over every obstacle, including the body of Paris, is necessary to produce the tragic outcome and the emotional contrasts and explosions. The mere death of Juliet, without such irony and mockery, would lead as naturally to the hero's own, not 'tonight' but a day or a week hence — after she has wakened! As things are, moreover, to Romeo, to the poet and his audience, the feud and fate or fortune are nearly identical. Nearly all that is needed to justify any tragic conclusion is adequate preparation; and this has been provided not only in premonition but in fulfilment as, twice before, the feud has bloody consequences — by the deaths of the Prince's kinsman and of Mercutio and Tybalt. Fortune's fool he is now more than ever as the Friar's message fails to reach him, and as he kills himself, Juliet being still alive. As Lemaître says of the *Œdipus*, 'C'est que le hasard en est la logique.'

12

If that is so, the rashness or impetuosity comes as a matter of course: without it the stars might lour but, not being defied, would bring down no disaster. In this audience I can no doubt presume an acquaintance with the *Toronto Quarterly* and possibly with my essay in the October number, on Reconciliation in Tragedy,[9]

[9] Reproduced, though enlarged, in the chapter of the book referred to above, p. 6, note 2.

in which I show that this particular sort of tragic fault, to be found in the heroes of other Shakespearean tragedies, such as *King Lear*, *Othello* and *Macbeth*, and in the ancient, such as the *Œdipus*, is often but a matter of tragic momentum. When the hero is positive, not negative, an actor, not merely a sufferer, and also virtuous and noble enough to keep our admiration and sympathy, how can he ordinarily come to grief at all if he be wholly prudent and discreet? In some measure, to be sure, for plausibility's sake, the tragic hero or heroine must be his or her own destiny, or seem to be so. Hence the Friar's moralizing about those stumbling who run fast, and on violent delights having violent ends. There he has a grain of justification — as Brabantio has when he warns Othello against the deceitfulness of Desdemona! He takes us with him, as he is meant to do, when, on Juliet's entry, he cries, like a poet,

> O, so light a foot
> Will ne'er wear out the everlasting flint.
>
> A lover may bestride the gossamer
> That idles in the wanton summer air,
> And yet not fall;

but not when he adds, like a monkish wiseacre:

> so light is vanity.

That is a little like Schück and Gervinus, Bodenstedt and Ulrici, who seem to have hearkened rather to him than to the hero and the heroine. It is in the interest of drama that the Friar is permitted to have his say, his point of view; in some small part it is even in the interest of drama that this humdrum prudence is given expression; but when he bids the young pair 'love moderately,' he does not fill the role of a chorus, or else the poet's efforts to arouse our emotions and call forth our whole sympathy for them would be defeated. He is the chorus only in so far as his moralizings and warnings have the effect of misgivings and forebodings, which contribute to the suspense.

A fault, moreover, implies in the catastrophe an act of justice; and for a satisfaction of that sense within us there is no place in this romantic tragedy of fate, but only for pity — and sympathy. All that is needed is that the catastrophe should be plausible and harmonious, in keeping with both our sense of reality and the nature of tragedy; and such it is. If Romeo, and Juliet too, did nothing at all to bring fate down upon their heads, they would not be the vital and positive natures that they have hitherto seemed to be, and the play would not be a tragedy. But in the circumstances they are not to blame, nor are they morbid or unbalanced, and you will surely excuse me from stopping to consider any notion so irrelevant as that they are impulsive, uninhibited Italians. What, then, of Macbeth and his Lady, in their impetuosity, who are Scotch? *Highland* Scotch, I suppose, Gaels, not dour Presbyterian Saxons. What *is* to the point has been said of late, though perhaps less truly, of the great love-story of the eighteenth century: 'Tout est simple dans *Manon,* comme le malheur et le plaisir, la jeunesse et l'amour.' Here are psychology and realism, not the stars or fortune, as in *Romeo and Juliet*. This is a novel, and as M. Suarès observes, classical in form; the other, a tragedy and certainly romantic. But masterpieces of literary art — novel or drama, classical or romantic, prose or verse — partake of the nature of poetry, even as 'all art,' according to Pater, 'constantly aspires towards the condition of music.' All masterpieces of fiction are akin. And *Manon* too is a poem, a triumphal hymn of love.

This before us is a finer, loftier one, with intenser emotional effect and less admixture of human frailty. The characters are less substantial and true to life but more vivid and convincing in themselves. We see them and hear them, to adapt Mr. Eliot's words, if we do not, on second thoughts, understand them. The height and intensity of emotional effect, however, is especially owing to the finer and more compelling rhythm. This is not merely in the verse but in the structure of the fable. Three times the feud asserts itself with fateful consequences, three times Romeo remembers his baleful stars, and once their malign influence is touched upon in the prologue. And there are verbal echoes, in Romeo's repeated recognition of a fate impending and his figure of the pilot and his bark. But the main musical effect is in the fluctuation, the swell and subsidence, which cannot be attained within the close and sober limits of prose. Within this storm of passion and the resultant harmony of effect Romeo and Juliet keep their individuality, none the less real because they stand for love contending with hatred, none the less human because they are not adequately motived, all the more vivid because placed in a situation not of their own making but touched by poetic power.

LECTURE II

The Maidens of Shakespeare's Prime

I

IN my last lecture I said that by Shakespeare the love of the sexes was not dramatized. I mean, as it has been by others. The dramatist did not follow the tradition of Ovid in his *ars amandi*, as developed before his own day by Ariosto, after it by Lope de Vega, or in his own time and country by Lyly, Chapman, Marston, and Fletcher. That is the conception of love as a game or a chase, the young man pursuing and the young woman fleeing — piteous or enticing when neglected, merry and scornful when wooed. Shakespeare's lovers are faithful and constant, and despite some proverbial sayings in his text, the women are not fickle. Neither does he follow the tradition of the medieval knightly code as Chapman and Fletcher do, whereby illicit relations are treated sympathetically. Nor does he anticipate the drama of the *beau monde* — the tragedy of love and honour, as in Corneille and Dryden, or the comedy of love in its follies and foibles, its pretenses and affectations, as in Congreve and Molière. Still less, of course, has he in common with the social drama of Browning in the *Blot in the Scutcheon* or of Dumas *fils* in the *Dame aux Camélias*, on the one hand, or of Hervieu, Ibsen and Shaw, Pinero and Granville-Barker, on the other. With him woman is not a victim of environment, an object of compassion; nor has she idiomatically or literally 'a mind of her own,' intent on living her own life, however much to our admiration, in defiance of the world.

In this last situation particularly there are the makings of drama, that is, conflict or opposition, the women being in some measure independent of the men. Shakespeare's are not. When in love they are not ordinarily the centres of dramatic interest; in fact, it is their peculiar excellence, Coleridge and Hazlitt agree, that they seem to exist only in their attachment to others. The men sometimes are jealous; the maidens and even the wives are not. They love, are lovable, and seek love in turn. The emotion is the centre, though not the sum, of their existence. Unlike the modern, they have no interest in their civic rights or in 'a career,' unlike Congreve's they have no social preoccupations or aspirations; unlike Lope's, on the one hand, they are no coquettes, and unlike Chapman's, on the other, no Guineveres; and a struggle like that of Corneille's Chimène, between love and her duty to family or parents, is (witness Juliet, Desdemona, and Imogen) quite beyond or beneath them. Apart from Shakespeare's and the contemporary dramatists' indifference to such a subject or want of a technique for treating it, it would to the Elizabethan taste have made them less romantic, let them seem less in love and more like life as it was;

and the open rupture of family ties by the three maidens just mentioned and the prevailing indifference to them shown by most of the others — once their affections are awakened — are no sign that the ties were outwardly stronger (though of course they were) and inwardly weaker than today.[1] One might as well conclude, from the evidence of all Elizabethan drama, that then falling in love at sight was much commoner than today. Still farther remote is a ruling passion like Iphigeneia's in Euripides and Racine, her devotion to the fatherland. Shakespeare's heroines are not emotionally sophisticated or intellectually exalted. Neither they nor their lovers are imbued with platonism or the Dantesque love-philosophy, unlike the ladies and cavaliers of the Italian Renaissance, and they engage in no subtilizing *ragionamenti d'amore*. There is something of that in the Sonnets, but not in his passionate theatre. Yet the heroines are ideal, not to say idyllic, are romantic and often naïve. They belong to another tradition than any hitherto mentioned, partly dramatic, as represented by Robert Greene and in some measure John Lyly, his predecessors, partly literary, as represented by Spenser in Una, Florimel, and Britomart, by Ariosto and the English and French chivalric and pastoral romances in prose and verse. They have no blots in their scutcheons

---

[1] Professor Schücking's inference, *Englische Studien*, vol. 62, pp. 191–2. — In so far as the family ties offer really dramatic material, a struggle, the Elizabethans, as we have seen in the previous lecture, were interested only in the external one; in so far as they are needed to complete the picture of life, the dramatists and the audience were engrossed in what was stirring in the foreground.

or bees in their bonnets, no novel opinions or individual aspirations; and they may now seem not only undramatic but hopelessly old-fashioned and insipid, unfitted for club-life and uninterested in 'uplift' or in lectures, even such as this one about them; but they are what can never be uninteresting, old-fashioned, or insipid — poetical.

2

In poetry is their origin and in poetry is their being, witness not only Juliet but Romeo; yet they are not vague or intangible because of having no private and individual stock of ideas, nor frail or insubstantial because of existing in their attachment to others. Poetically conceived, poetical in their utterance, they do not go in for poetry themselves like the faithful shepherdesses in the pastorals. None of them meditates the thankless or the grateful Muse. Not aware that they are poetical, they are therefore all the more so; and in their substance and their manner they are very natural human beings, with girlish tastes, interests, and appetites. Though not so in name, they are English rather than French, Italian, or Illyrian; and like the women of their own country today, keep something of the spirit of a girl as the men keep something of the spirit of a boy.[2] 'They are ideal,' to use Mr. Murry's phrase, 'in the most humane sense of the word, an enchanting and attainable perfection of the real.' They are not lost

---

[2] Cf. *Times Literary Supplement*, Feb. 28, 1935, a review of *The English Smile*, by Christen Hansen.

in visions wide like Madeleine in the *Eve of St. Agnes*. Not one of them is a Genevieve, or Christabel, or damsel with a dulcimer — on honeydew they have *not* fed nor drunk the milk of Paradise. Not one of them is too bright or good for human nature's daily food. Portia, the fairy princess of Belmont, and Miranda, the fairy princess of the desert isle, what would not Shelley or Tennyson have made of them? But neither of them is a witch of Atlas in her cavern or a Lady of Shalott in her castle. Nor is either endowed with a moral or allegorical significance — a Spenserian Phaedria singing and laughing in her magic boat, or a Dantesque Leah singing and picking flowers on the mountain, or Rachel gazing in her glass. Though love is to be their chief interest in life, it is the human, earthly, fairly sensible sort, in its simplicity and purity; it is, moreover, not their interest from the outset. They do not brood or languish. None of Shakespeare's young women is in love with love like Romeo; for this is long before the day of Keats or Rossetti. Matrimony is an honour that they dream not of, though at a touch they yield.

They are more like the heroines of Greene and Sir Philip Sidney than of any other, though both more ideal and also more real, sharing with Greene's women traits that should reassure us. Once awakened, they are willing to be wooed, to the point of inviting it, and in some ways they half take the initiative (but not, as Mr. Shaw thinks, altogether) or await it eagerly, though with humour and self-possession. This forwardness, says Mr. Shaw and, apparently, Mr. F. L.

Lucas,[3] is realism; women do the wooing in life, though they are not supposed to, but so artfully that they are not caught at it by the unsuspecting males. The spider, declares our contemporary Voltaire, entraps the fly. In these days of anarchy, in morals and manners both — in these days of matriarchy, when books, plays, music, lectures, magazine articles, and advertisements are written or presented mainly for and in large measure by the women — there may seem to be some basis for that notion; there are even on record, to support him in his contention, the advances made by aspiring, eugenic-minded women to — of all persons — Mr. Shaw (formidable fly!) himself. But that does not make the practice usual or acceptable in Shakespeare's day. Nor does it permit us, with Professor Matthews, to 'deduce the dramatist's opinion that women are readier to take the first step in love-making than is ordinarily supposed.'[4] For Shakespeare and his audience it is not a realistic but a romantic quality, though a fairly substantial one; at bottom, of course, women want to be wooed quite as much as men want to woo them, and only propriety interferes. It interfered, certainly, in Shakespeare's day. The young women's frankness with their lovers in speech is like their following them up in boys' clothing, frequent not only in Shakespeare but in Elizabethan drama before and after him, not only in the drama and novel of the Italian and the Spanish Renaissance but in

---

3 *Man and Superman*, 'Epistle Dedicatory'; *Tragedy* (1935), pp. 114–115.
4 *Shakespeare as a Playwright* (1913), pp. 223, 380.

Spenser and Ariosto and Boiardo, who cannot be considered realistic except when in comic vein: and in story the venture was appealing, even in cases that warranted it, just because it ran counter to custom, was opposed to probability and to taste. As we noticed yesterday, high romance is not propriety carried to extremes, but overridden. Meeting the men half way or more, dressing in boys' clothing to follow them up, falling in love at sight beforehand, or, as in Desdemona's case, losing one's heart to a negro — these doings are all on the same dizzy level. The silly and the vulgar do the like, but with a difference. Propriety — reticence and reserve — are excellent things, but above all as a measure; and the love that breaks their bonds — perfect love casteth out fear — is stronger. Certainly it is more bewitching. In life itself the beautiful and graceful woman can do much that a man does, and by man's dress and demeanour even heighten her charms; in poetry she can still more easily if, to use Hazlitt's words, 'taught by the force of feeling when to forego the forms of propriety for the essence of it'; and here is a time-honoured example of the way that poetry obeys her own laws and secures the effect of reality even in contradicting it. The difference between realism and romance is — that between our militant feminists or Mr. Shaw's wooers and Shakespeare's ladies in love! It is because Shakespeare's are romantic that they are not reticent, as it is because they are really romantic that they do not coquet.

3

Something the same may be said of the wit and humour in the woman when her heart first opens. Like meeting the man half way or more, and in his costume, it is a delicate thing to handle: either her intentions may seem too serious — or not serious enough. But nothing could more reassure us concerning the flesh-and-blood reality of the lovers, and bring the ideal more gracefully and happily down to earth.

Merriment serves also another purpose, characteristic of great art, that of substitution and suggestion. It replaces the voluptuous and luscious. Despite their frankness, lovers keep their distance both in fact and in thought, as, when (like these) of one accord, in life they seldom do. Shakespeare's are simple and passionate but, though substantial enough, seldom what today would be called sensuous. In the dialogue there are few occasions for a caress or embrace, and there is little dilating upon the sensations that these naturally and ordinarily produce. Mr. Granville-Barker, who has discussed the subject with the perception of a dramatist and producer, but, here as it seems to me, a rather too modern one, thinks that there were no caresses because women's parts were played by boys. But by boys or men they had been played for thousands of years, and would the audience even think of such a thing as their being played by women? Tom Coryat, the Elizabethan, in Venice, wondered at finding that women there played women's parts as successfully as men. How much more likely that the spell of illusion would be broken, if at all, by the incongruity when the Juliet of *Measure for Measure* appears with her new-born babe in her arms; or when Hermione, presently to give birth to a child, appeals to the King, to have women with her in prison,

>   for, you see,
> My plight requires it!

or when Lady Macbeth bids the spirits

> > Come to my woman's breasts
> And take my milk for gall;

or declares she has given suck and knows

> How tender 'tis to love the babe that milks me;

or when her husband bids her bring forth men children only! Because of the boy actor, then, were all such pathetic or tragic moments endangered or spoiled? Moreover, if such were the attitude or disposition of the audience, there must at serious sentimental moments be no caresses at all; the rarer and more unusual they were, the more likely to provoke hilarity; and yet Mr. Granville-Barker admits that in *Antony and Cleopatra* the dialogue provides for two embraces, ' it may be three.' If such were the attitude or disposition of the audience, there would be more laughter at the first embrace than the third, and at the third than the twentieth. To me it seems more probable that the question before us is solely one of dramatic art, not the scenic or histrionic; and except when the actor was unskilful, the audience surrendered to the illusion, properly forgetting at the theatre the conformation of the actual bodies in skirts before them. The explanation given is too much like those other mechanistic, materialistic ones, on which I have dwelt elsewhere,[5] — the long rhetorical, lyrical, and frankly self-revealing speeches and the quiet scene-endings as owing to the projection of the stage into the amphitheatrical house and to the want of a front curtain; or, in ancient drama, the lack of disguise and of violent action on the stage as owing to the classical costume and the high-heeled cothurnus; and the unities (which, in a sense, are observed even in the *Iliad* and the *Odyssey*) as owing to the chorus. If these features of drama were not primarily a matter of stage conveniences or limitations but of Elizabethan or classical literary tradition and taste, in which, as generally, dramatist and public coincided, this under discussion must be much the same. If climacteric scene-endings were desired, a curtain could easily have been procured — the fact is that sometimes they are provided for without it, as in Act II, Scene iv of the Folio *King Lear*, by the actors themselves; and if luscious and voluptuous demonstrations on the stage were desired, and the other sex was not permitted by the authorities on the stage, amends could have been made in the language, as in Fletcher's day they were. Luscious and voluptuous demonstrations on the stage were not desired; and art, inclining to substitution

[5] Cf. above, p. 6, note 2, and *Shakespeare Studies*, pp. 377-83.

rather than imitation or reproduction, provided an equivalent — in Cleopatra, as Mr. Granville-Barker himself says, 'wit, malice, or subtle mischief,' though this was simply because she was a woman, not because she was played by a boy.[6]

Without a wit combat, indeed, or (as sometimes is the case) the comic presentation of innocence and naïveté, what should the dramatist, as we have come to know him, do for a situation? He has, as we have seen, renounced the ordinary and natural difficulties and misunderstandings between lovers, such as thoroughgoing coquetry, difference in point of view, or a struggle between love and duty; and in the way of realism there is left him little scope. 'Twofold silence is the song of love,' in the north, at least, though the words quoted are those of a poet half Italian.

> Verbosa gaudet Venus loquela,

sings Catullus; but Shakespeare knew no racial psychology, and makes his lovers talkative because his drama, like the ancient, is rather that of speech than of pantomime and gesture — of speech in all its abundance, and with him the exhilaration of love may properly take the form of wit and humour. Was not Venus (or Aphrodite) the goddess of laughter too? Now with wit combats heartfelt caresses, or the vivid imagining of them either, need not interfere; but it is a curious fact that in the theatre, not only in the ages before the ad-

---

6 For Mr. Granville-Barker's views see *Companion to Shakespeare Studies*, pp. 54–56, and his Prefaces *passim*.

vent of women upon the stage but in the less than three centuries since, little room has been given to either the reality or the fiction. In the best Elizabethan drama, Shakespearean or not, erotic satisfaction was mainly by way of smutty jokes; but these were for the most part on the lips of the low-class, the minor characters, not of the lovers; and romance was kept intact, unsullied and untroubled. In the Jacobean there was more voluptuousness; and in Restoration comedy modesty and shame nearly forsook the stage. But so did romance, and what little is there can hold up its head. There is much freer speaking on the stage both about and between the sexes, but in the Congrevian *Comedy of Manners*, as in Fletcher's, nearly all the license is in the spirit of jest, meagrely mingled with emotion; and for the romantic wooings in Shakespeare we have the bargaining or proviso scenes, which are wit combats again, such as the celebrated one between Millamant and Mirabell in *The Way of the World*. 'Well, you ridiculous thing, you, I'll have you — I won't be kissed, nor I won't be thanked — here, kiss my hand though' — and that is as close to the bewitching creature as Mirabell ever gets. There are moments of 'warmth,' as it was called, in Van Brugh's *Relapse*, for instance, and Farquhar's *Beaux' Stratagem*, but in connexion with attempted seductions, not with legitimate passion. And even today, when there is such unabashed liberty in poem and in novel, there is, in high-class drama, no love scene that I can remember which reads as if Rossetti or Swinburne had written it. How the actors present it is not the question, but only the text itself; and generally merriment is mingled with the wooing unless there be some other dramatic ingredient, such as a tragic misgiving or a clash in points of view. In Mr. Maugham's *Circle*, for instance, the wooing is highly romantic in spirit and serious in purpose, but mostly by way of jest and mirth. Mere passion, with the accompanying physical manifestations, is, however healthy, either too simple and undramatic for the stage or else too offensive to that public sense of decorum which has outlasted the private, and — miraculously — still asserts itself in the theatre long after it has been renounced in print. Individually we are willing enough to read or think of what, five hundred together, we are not so willing to see. In the pit some would chafe, in the gallery some would jeer, but with book in hand we are in no danger of being put out of countenance.

> Chastes sont les oreilles
> Encor que les yeux soient fripons,

declares Voltaire, quoting La Fontaine, and reminding his readers of the contrast between the pruriency of classical Roman satire and the decency of the comedy.[7]

Endearments of another sort, however, mingle freely with the wit. As in the Capulets' garden, the twofold song of love is sung. The psychological motive or justification of the passion may be somewhat lacking, but as Mr. Murry says, 'the poet does not profess to show how it happens; he does something far more difficult;

---
7 Voltaire, Lèttre 19 (Sur la comédie), vol. 22.

he convinces us that it has happened. He makes his lovers say the simplest and divinest things; they seem to drop sunbeams from their lips . . . When Orlando says of Rosalind that she is "just as high as his heart," when Rosalind says that "men have died from time to time and worms have eaten them, but not for love " . . . we recognize the speech of love as surely as the old prophets recognized the voice of the Lord.[8]

4

Ideal, then, and to the point of being idyllic; witty and humorous or innocent and naïve, and often all at once and together, without much in the way of individual opinions concerning life or love in general, and without any wholly characteristic attitude towards the situation in the play; ready to be wooed, and many of them to the point themselves of wooing and of following up their lovers as boys, yet nearly all, as we shall see, self-sacrificing and some even self-renouncing: how can poetic and romantic maidens so similar be easily distinguished and vividly appreciated? Each of them has all the virtues and nearly all the charms; and as long as Mrs. Jameson confines herself to naming and enumerating these we make no progress. Of love's language they are unquestionably mistresses, but have they voices of their own? The earliest real critic of Shakespeare in France, himself a great poet and romancer, is of the opinion that they have not. Adapting but contradicting

[8] *Countries of the Mind*, p. 17.

the words which Pope applied to Shakespeare's characters in general, Chateaubriand avers (and Tolstoy supports him) that if one effaced their names or closed one's eyes one would not know which of them has spoken. 'They have the same smile,' says he, ' the same look, the same tone of voice.' The internal and external likenesses are so great that the critic could not discern the difference, for it lies just where it would escape a foreigner — in their accents. Particularly a critic accustomed, like Chateaubriand, to Corneille, Racine, and Molière; a critic who expected to find the character a structure rather than a poetic evocation, and in an action that, even though inherited, had been fashioned quite anew, so as to be the expression of character, less an Italian *novella* turned into dramatic verse. But however it be with smile or look, Shakespeare's young women have not the same voice. Racine's Phèdre and Roxane, jealous and infatuated women, have not either, the Cretan's tone being languid and the Oriental's imperious and ruthless; yet in both the centre of interest lies within. The character is to be found in the lady's speeches taken together, rather than in any one. The character of Rosalind or of Imogen — and there is the difference between the psychological and the more poetical and imaginative method — is to be found in any and every one; and it is while Mrs. Jameson, Hazlitt, and Coleridge are *listening*, instead of analysing and ratiocinating, that they come to know their natures, as we do, if we have ears as good. Nor are their smiles and looks the same. They must have somewhat different traits, of course, or different combinations of them, otherwise their voices would not be different. On the printed page a voice can only be suggested — by the turn of the thought or the structure of the sentence, by melody and rhythm; for melody and rhythm in prose or verse are not, like those in music, independent of a meaning. And their differences in mood and temper we shall presently undertake to make out for ourselves.

Curiously enough, another fine French critic, a generation later, takes the converse position, that Shakespeare's women, like his other characters, are better individualized than Corneille's and Racine's. Not only must he have had an ear more responsive to English idiom and rhythm, and to Shakespeare's differentiating use of them, he must also have been more appreciative of the Shakespearean abundance and delicacy of expression. 'Racine's lovers,' says Mézières, 'all breathe the same sighs to heaven, and their mistresses repeat the conventional theme of elevated passion.' Taken together, these details make an interesting character, but, as in Jane Austen's attractive women, are often not interesting in themselves. In Shakespeare's they are. Indeed, the incidental touches, not necessary to the action, which in the characterization, because of the little developed dramatic quality, are fairly frequent, must needs be interesting to justify their presence. Rosalind's commonsense attitude towards Arcadian sentimentality and melancholy and her interest in Orlando because her father had loved his, like Perdita's notion of what is natural and what artificial in flowers, lead to nothing in the sequel yet are both unconventional touches and also significant ones. What is a superfluity in the external structure may even contribute to the illusion.

5

Discussion of an artist's work, however, is only a stepping-stone to appreciation, which depends on direct contact with the work itself. Today we shall glance at some of the young women of Shakespeare's early prime, or rather listen to them; and in chronological order — Portia of Belmont, Beatrice, Rosalind, Viola.

Portia is the stateliest, the most nearly a fine lady of them all, for Viola is too much a slip of a girl. As befits her position in the world, mistress of her own household, she has most self-reliance and dignity; and in the role of judge she has these qualities and a tone of authority too. Yet she has almost the spirit of a schoolgirl as, putting on a disguise, she undertakes the expedition to Venice, and as she plays the trick of the rings. Here is a clear case of what the Renaissance critics and many of the dramatists would have called failing to keep decorum, that is, consistency in outward deportment according to one's rank and station. Racine might not have considered her a lady, nor, possibly, Molière. Racine might have applied to her what Professor Frye, his great admirer, has said of Shakespeare's high-born maidens in general, 'those long-legged, loose-mouthed hoydens in rompers.' And a lady certainly Portia is not if judged wholly by the standards of French tragedy (or comedy either), is not of the *beau monde*, a woman of fashion. Thoughts of society and its decrees, reputation and decorum, never occur to her, as they do not, except momentarily, to Shakespeare's other women; the words *ma gloire*, though now and then they might be, are never on her lips. She belongs and is in a world of poetry — Shakespeare's Belmont, Shakespeare's Venice — larger, airier than the *beau monde*, and has an unconscious natural dignity of her own. As a lady she is like Shakespeare's gentlemen, even his kings and queens; and like English gentlemen and ladies nowadays, who preserve their privileges as human beings and not infrequently unbend. On occasion they jest and disport themselves, as in seventeenth-century French tragedy they never, and in comedy seldom or scarcely, do.

The lady of Belmont breathes and moves freely, a thoroughbred. How proud and princely she is in the surrender of her heart and her fortunes to her wooer, and of even him for a time — for the first days of their happiness — in the overruling interests of friendship! She has only a touch of even that playful coquetry we have found in Juliet, just enough to satisfy the woman in her:

> I could teach you
> How to choose right, but then I am forsworn;
> So will I never be; so may you miss me;
> But if you do, you'll make me wish a sin,
> That I had been forsworn.

Yet on hearing his disquieting news she at once bids him ' away to Venice to your friend.' ' First go with me to church ' — that, like Juliet or any other of Shakespeare's young women, she is not the one to forget — but even so she bids him make haste, and not to the altar,

> O love, dispatch all business, and be gone!

Juliet would have had to struggle with herself to say it; and that Portia does not say it lightly is apparent from her words before the choice of the casket:

> I pray you, tarry. Pause a day or two
> Before you hazard; for, in choosing wrong,
> I lose your company; therefore forbear a while.

After such an invitation who would not have tarried, except where time is as precious as on Shakespeare's stage? And it is amid the same high considerations, above merely personal cravings and legal requirements, that her mind moves as she plays the judge:

> Then must the Jew be merciful . . .

> The quality of mercy is not strain'd.
> It droppeth as the gentle rain from heaven
> Upon the place beneath.

> It is not so express'd; but what of that?
> 'Twere good you do so much for charity.

There the spiritual elevation of her appears (at least for one who has memories of Irving and Ellen Terry) as she stands before the stooping, insistent Jew —

> On what compúlsion must I? téll me thát.
>
> Is it sò nóminated in the bónd?
>
> I cannot fínd it; 'tis nòt ín the bónd.

The angelical syllables of mercy and charity are Greek to him, not Hebrew; to have weight with him they must be denied their nature, set down in black and white, signed and sealed. And how well she plays the part, truly a Daniel come to judgment, with the dignity, serenity, and swift precision (but now heightened) that she manifested in arranging and settling matters after receiving the news at Belmont. Like most feigning in Shakespeare — Hamlet's, Rosalind's, Viola's — it is of a part not quite foreign to her nature. The law she administers and manipulates is not good law nor ever was, and in the rigour wherewith it is turned against him who has called upon it, there is more of justice, indeed, than of mercy; but neither consideration is meant to count with us here. To Shakespeare and his theatre Portia is Themis herself, Astraea returned to earth.[9]

And yet 'the whole happy virtue' of her character is not in the traits but, to use Mr. Granville-Barker's words, 'in the melody of her speech.' Without the traits, there would of course be no meaning and therefore no melody — the doctrine of Miss Stein and the others who freely dispense with sense, does not here apply; but it is the melody that gives them effect.

[9] I am here presenting views more amply developed in the chapter on Shylock, in my *Shakespeare Studies*.

And Portia's voice (not Ellen Terry's merely) rings clear as crystal, true as silver. The mercy speech is her aria, her bravura piece, but it is the same voice there as in the recitative when she accepts Bassanio as the successful suitor. How it peals out upon our ears, despite some little tinkle of euphuism! Of this there has been plenty in her opening colloquy with Nerissa and afterwards — balance and antithesis, pun, paradox, and epigram, ' sentence ' or aphorism — for is she not a fine lady of the Renaissance, fully armed? — and there is something of it even in her higher poetic moments, here as in the judgment scene. The euphuism does not separate her from our world — not the Portia of my memory, at any rate — and now as I read her words, which will never perish, I hear, as most of you cannot, the voice that did:

> You see me, Lord Bassanio, where I stand,
> Such as I am. Though for myself alone
> I would not be ambitious in my wish,
> To wish myself much better; yet, for you
> I would be trebled twenty times myself,
> A thousand times more fair, ten thousand times
> More rich;
> That only to stand high in your account,
> I might in virtues, beauties, livings, friends,
> Exceed account. But the full sum of me
> Is sum of — something, which, to term in gross,
> Is an unlesson'd girl, unschool'd, unpractis'd;
> Happy in this, she is not yet so old
> But she may learn; happier than this,

> She is not bred so dull but she can learn;
> Happiest of all is that her gentle spirit
> Commits itself to yours to be directed,
> As from her lord, her governor, her king.
> Myself and what is mine to you and yours
> Is now converted. But now I was the lord
> Of this fair mansion, master of my servants,
> Queen o'er myself; and even now, but now,
> This house, these servants, and this same myself
> Are yours, my lord; I give them with this ring;

An unlesson'd girl, unschool'd, unpractis'd — is she that? Yet it is she that is speaking, not the dramatist, and to her husband. For love is humble, at the outset. At such a moment, if by fate it had been vouchsafed to her, Elizabeth Tudor herself, in all her imperious and impudent majesty, might so have spoken. Portia is, indeed, without experience, living in such distant seclusion; yet of experience, as history shows us — witness Joan of Arc, Catherine II, Elizabeth herself — women have no need. How quickly the secluded Juliet and Imogen and Perdita rise to the occasion, to the exigencies of full-blown womanhood! And of the veracity of the utterance there is no question.

> You sée me, Lórd Bassánio, where I stánd,
> Súch as I ám.

There are her dignity and serenity, her even flow of thought and syllable, with none of the flutter or disorder of young love, of first love, but as clear and spacious in her view of things as when afterwards she presides over the tribunal. *Lord* Bassanio she calls him, though now he is her own: her Elizabethan decorum, her natural, unschool'd dignity demand it. In Shakespeare young people lose or abandon their hearts to each other as in real life they seldom did or do; yet they keep the forms of polite address in a day when there was still some vestige of reticence and reserve, and the equivalent of Mr. and Miss had not been done away with. For them there are intimacies still in store. Even at a later day, Fielding's Sophia murmurs to Tom, her hand fast in his, 'What would Mr. Jones *have* me say?' *Mr.* Jones!

6

Beatrice is the most mettlesome — ' coy and wild as a haggard [untamed falcon] of the rock.' And yet she is more of the *beau monde* than any of the others, and is Shakespeare's equivalent for Congreve's Millamant. Only, her wit is not employed in coquetry or frivolity like Millamant's, nor for that matter in wooing like Juliet's and Rosalind's, but in what is, or once upon a time was, a lady's chief art and sport and crowning glory — conversation. (Now, like the men, they ' do things '; now they swear and swap stories, but cannot talk!) Ultimately, no doubt, this game of wit is a kind of coquetry, too, being directed mostly at the men, though in the form of banter and persiflage, a coquetry inverted. Benedick is its chief mark — it strikes where it doth love. But of this last she is not yet aware, and the great moments in her life are when she becomes so, on learning that he is in love with her, and on hearing in the church innocent Hero accused by Claudio. Then by her pleasantry she is deserted or she abandons it. At the one moment she flings off her pride:

> What fire is in mine ears? Can this be true?

> And, Benedick, love on. I will requite thee,
> Taming my wild breast to thy loving hand.

At the other, she rushes to the rescue. As Hero falls in a swoon she cries:

> Why, how now, cousin, wherefore sink you down?

and when Benedick, avowing his love, begs her to let him prove it, she bursts out like a pistol shot,

> Kill Claudio.

For she is mettlesome to the core, and the finger-tips: her love, like her hate, which is born of it, breaks out in jets and gushes.

Her voice is that of the mocking-bird, now sharp, now sweet, and no one was ever more vivacious or highstrung. At times her wit is for us too personal and satirical, though of the sort delighted in at the palace of the Duke of Urbino if we are to judge of that by Castiglione's Book of the Courtier, and at Windsor and Richmond (from what we know of them) in Shakespeare's day. (Elizabeth's tongue ran unbridled, certainly.) But the spirit of it, the rhythm and exhilaration of it, will never grow old. How impetuous the raillery, and merrily impatient the repetition, in her first inquiry after Benedick:

> I pray you, how many hath he kill'd and eaten in these wars? But how many hath he kill'd? for indeed I promised to eat all of his killing.

So she comes tripping and dancing, and pirouettes; so her wit, like all art at its best, approaches 'the condition of music.' And when she and Benedick are in love with each other the word-play of both becomes lighter and is today more acceptable. 'By this hand, I love thee,' quoth Benedick. 'Use it for my love some other way than swearing by it,' is her sprightly and pointed retort, in allusion to his weapon. Even before that, ere a new world has opened up round about her, she betrays, in the midst of her banter, despite her disclaimers, a sympathetic comprehension of love and wistful interest in it. When Hero and Claudio are first engaged that sweet lady seems to her too reticent:

> Speak, cousin; or if you cannot, stop his mouth with a kiss, and let not him speak neither.

D. PEDRO. In faith, lady, you have a merry heart.
BEAT. Yea, my lord; I thank it, poor fool, it keeps on the windy side of care. My cousin tells him in his ear that he is in her heart.
CLAUD. And so she doth, cousin.

And then, with a mocking sigh, she rejoins, in a generous envy:

Good Lord, for alliance. Thus every one goes to the world [i.e. gets married] but I, and I am sunburnt [out in the cold]. I may sit in a corner and cry heigh-ho for a husband!

Don Pedro offers to procure her one; and upon a free-spoken, Elizabethan repartee, he declares that she was born in a merry hour.

No, sure, my lord, my mother cried; but then there was a star danc'd, and under that was I born.

And that is where I like her best, when she flutters up into the air upon iridescent wings, her pleasantry, like Mercutio's, and Falstaff's too at times, turning to fantasy. But audiences nowadays would not; to the poetry of wit their ears are even less attuned than to that of sentiment.

7

Rosalind is the heartiest, the most abundant and exuberant. In her, for once, Aphrodite, goddess of love and laughter, flew up into the North, and by her if not by others the 'laureate of love' wins his laurels. Beatrice when most moved contracts to seriousness; Rosalind unfolds and expands. For her wit has no trace of a sting in it — like her frown, which Orlando fears would kill him, — 'By this hand,' she, in her disguise, reassures him, 'it will not kill a fly.' Wit and humour are both the mask and the indirect utterance of her passion, the effervescence of her happiness. Indeed, love and merriment are in her fairly inseparable, even when happiness is still in doubt. 'But is all this for your father?' Celia asks her cousin when after the first sight of Orlando she is in the dumps.

>No, some of it is for my child's father,

which in Elizabeth Bergner's screen version has been sentimentally blunted and flattened into 'my father's child.' And this glorious, romantic reunion of love and laughter Shakespeare has facilitated by the conventions of disguise and impersonation. As Rosalind and Orlando pretend that in her man's clothing she is Rosalind, she plays only a part that she feels, and eagerly notes as he woos her how much — and says mockingly, how little — he feels the part he plays. Fact and fiction here merge, and her joy in the fact overflows in her merriment over the fiction.

This is a remarkable case of an improbable convention being employed to enrich the situation, to broaden the emotional range; for it is the high ambition and privilege of art not to reproduce reality but without conspicuously offending against it to enlarge its confines. Her disguise is like the feigning of Hamlet, whereby, under the cover of madness, he can, as he bides his time, say out what he thinks and feels. It is like the convention of calumny credited, whereby the spirit of jealous vengeance coils round Othello's trustful love. And there, and often elsewhere in art, the end justifies the means. As we have seen already, the spirit of wit and humour, and the taking of the initiative by a newly enamoured but sweet and innocent young woman, though rightly treated, they heighten the romantic effect, decidedly imperil it; but here both are given full warrant by a device that is improbability itself. Orlando, for whom to see her was to love her, a day or two ago, would surely know her in any costume conceivable, to their days' end. But without the armour of disguise Rosalind could not profit by full knowledge on her part or by ignorance on his; and, certain of his love though she has not yet received a proposal, she would not be in a position, as she is, to coax him into making it, under the mocking eyes of Celia, in words that are enough to pull the soul out of his body:

Come, woo me, woo me: for now I am in a holiday humour and like enough to consent. What would you say to me now, an I were your very very Rosalind?

Spoken in skirts and stomacher, at a time when, off the stage, women no more laid bare their hearts than they then did their bodies, such words would never do. Spoken in disguise or without, by the enlightened and enfranchised female of today, they would do well enough but lack their startling charm. They would lend themselves to psychology, not drama. By the convention of disguise Rosalind is given the advantages of merriment and audacity without the disadvantages, and thus what a breadth of emotion she, and we in turn, enjoy! Before taking on this role of Rosalind the beloved, she, as the youth instructed by his lovelorn uncle, is sceptical — Orlando has not the symptoms —

A lean cheek, which you have not; a blue eye and sunken, which you have not . . .

and she merrily enumerates the many signs of careless desolation that she half-ruefully misses. The wooing begun, she cries out, for the pure joy of saying it, ' Am I not your Rosalind? ' flinging her arms wide in her hose and doublet, but thereupon, in her pretended person in skirts, refuses him. He then, in his own person, is for dying:

No faith, die by attorney. The poor world is almost six thousand years old, and in all this time there was not any man died in his own person, videlicit, in a love-cause. Troilus . . . Leander . . . But thése are àll líes. Mén have diéd from time to time, and wórms have eáten them, but nót for lóve.

His right Rosalind Orlando would not have of this mind; she is far enough from it, to the point of letting Celia play the priest and marry them; and before the scene is over, her counterfeiting is pretty nearly like that when she swoons at the sight of the bloody napkin. ' For these two hours, Rosalind,' sighs Orlando, ' I will leave thee.' ' Alas, dear love,' she whimpers, in her hose and doublet, ' I cannot láck thee twò hoúrs! ' It is a jest between them, and another jest for herself and Celia, and underneath no jest at all.

Her voice — words of my own here fail me and I have recourse to the infallible Hazlitt: ' How full of voluble, laughing grace! ' At her best, with her lover, she talks prose, like Beatrice but unlike Portia and

Viola, in whom wit and humour yield priority to the lyric or sentimental mood. For these impetuous, effervescent spirits, in the midst of verse, prose alone will do, with its untrammelled liberties of wording and of rhythm; and how marvelously the medium responds to them both! It is poetry, but neither bastard prose nor free verse; it is drama, as it falls in with the pulsations of human utterance, laughing or rallying, but coaxing — half teasing, half caressing. 'For ever and a day,' murmurs Orlando.

Ros. Say 'a day,' without the 'ever.' No, no, Orlando. Men are April when they woo, December when they wed; maids are May when they are maids, but the sky changes when they are wives. I will be more jealous of thee than a Barbary cock-pigeon over his hen, more clamorous than a parrot against rain, more new-fangled than an ape, more giddy in my desires than a monkey. I will weep for nothing, like **Diana** in the fountain, and I will do that when you are dispos'd to be merry. I will laugh like a hyen, and that when thou art inclin'd to sleep.

Orl. But will my Rósalind do so?
Ros. By my life, she will do as I do.

What a change and fresh precipitate running start at 'I will be more jealous of thee than a Barbary cock-pigeon over his hen,' what giddiness of rhythm in 'more giddy in my desires than a monkey,' and what a curvet and toss of the mane in 'By my life, she will do as I do'!

One of the most charming of Rosalind's traits is her

affection for Celia, and no speech ever expressed more happily the affection that runs over into another:

O coz, coz, coz, my pretty little coz, that thou didst know how many fathom deep I am in love.

Repetitions such as these are as characteristic of her voluble exuberance as her rhythms. Beatrice has repetitions of her own, but high spirits rather than affection are behind them.

8

Viola is the sweetest. She belongs to the tradition of Julia in the *Two Gentlemen of Verona*, who follows her faithless lover in page's costume and, thus disguised, enters his service; and in this capacity, like Julia, she is his emissary of love to another woman. Here is the clearest case in Shakespeare's earlier period of the self-forgetfulness and self-effacingness that reaches its culmination in Imogen and Hermione. All of his young heroines are men's notions of women — living for love, and once they have found it, finding life without it nearly (yet not wholly) worthless. This love of Viola's and the later heroines' is a farther-reaching, transcendental sort, its own reward, which, Shakespeare's men, like all others, though even at their best they themselves never attain to it, in women admire. That Shakespeare considered it unmanly is improbable: did he not indite the seventy-first sonnet, which is full of it? Like the other Elizabethans until the time of Fletcher and Massinger, like the ancients before him, he seems to have thought that attributing the quality to the hero, in whom the interest centres, would relax the tension of the situation.

Even his women of this sort, however, keep plenty of the spice of human nature; and like Imogen and Hermione, Viola is not wan or watery-eyed. The beauty of her rival Olivia she is not above endeavouring to see for herself; and like Imogen and Hermione, she has wit and humour, though of a quiet sort. This is one of the great things in Shakespeare, that, though utterly devoted, beyond recovery, none of his women in love is touched with the sickliness of sainthood or the meagreness of martyrdom — that none for mere love could pine away or die by her own hand. Viola's pleasantry is of no use to her in love-making, for until the end the Duke is not aware of her identity; but it serves her in answering up to Maria and the Clown and in considering the question of Olivia's being in love with her. And how characteristic the difference between the female page's

> Poor lady, she were better love a dream

and Rosalind's remark in the midst of her reproaches to the cruel and coquettish shepherdess Phoebe —

> 'Od's my little life,
> I think she means to tangle my eyes too.

Rosalind has no bleeding wound to awaken her sympathy, nor does Phoebe like Olivia deserve it; otherwise the situation is the same, for Rosalind too is tender-hearted. The contrast, therefore, is striking.

Her voice is that of the flute, plaintive though mellow. Undertaking to prove to her master that women are 'as true at heart as we,' she cites the case of her father's daughter who never told her love, but pined away, smiling at grief, and then asks him, without betraying herself,

> Was not this love indeed?

She knows, if he doesn't; but even the highest love must needs crave some faint shadow of recognition, else it would deny its nature. With the emotion she proves herself, in these shy and appealing ways, as despite his preoccupation even her master notices, intimately, if not immediately, familiar. When the Duke inquires how she likes the song, she answers,

> It gives a very echo to the seat
> Where love is thron'd.

'My life upon 't,' cries the Duke,

> thine eye
> Hath stay'd upon some favour that it loves,
> Hath it not, boy?

> A little, by your favour.

And even because she is not weakly despairing, her reticence has finer effect and point.

If, then, our analysis has been of any avail these young women have voices; and were I anything of a reader, you would yesterday and today have been hearing them. Chateaubriand is wrong and Mézières is right. A contemporary French critic, M. Schlumberger, goes still farther than the latter, and says the Shakespearean characters have bodies, too, as the Cornelian and Racinian have not. Exactly what he means is not perfectly clear; but apparently it is that they have many more definite and concrete ties with the ordinary world about them, and betray their everyday tastes and habits. They are less typical, more individualized. But this, as we have seen, is mainly through their speech — it is thus that they take on bodies, that we both hear and see them. One must be careful, to be sure, remembering the controversy concerning the colour of Lady Macbeth's hair. Concerning such matters we can know nothing except when the dramatist informs us, which is seldom. But it is impossible to conceive of Rosalind as thin and meagre, of Beatrice or Portia or Viola as plump or stout. It is impossible also to conceive of Celia as so tall as Rosalind, Hero so tall as Beatrice, Nerissa or Jessica so tall as Portia, or Viola as Olivia. In most of these cases, indeed, the dramatist has informed us that they are not. From the time of Lyly and Greene or earlier there were in comedy a pair of players for the established pair of young women in love, one taller than the other, one blonde and the other brown or 'black.' The contrast, obviously, was demanded by the stage; and the poet, naturally, availed himself of it. And it was proper enough that, other things being equal, the leading role — the queenlier, the more passionate and the wittier — should be given to the taller actor. Or if, as in *Twelfth Night,* the sweet and pathetic role should for once be the leading one, it would still be given to the smaller actor. But the difference in the lines was not mainly a matter of company organization: the roles were not written merely for the players. No dramatist of great imaginative power can confine himself within such limits; or expect to realize his creation on the boards. The roles were written for the play and for the other roles; the leading female one, in particular, to contrast with the secondary, though profiting by the contrast provided in the company personnel. In both speech and aspect Rosalind and Celia, Beatrice and Hero, Portia and Nerissa, throw each other into relief. It is thus, in part, that we both hear and see them.

And yet — here is some justification for Chateaubriand — they are alike because they themselves, as well as the roles they fill, are the development of a tradition. In form and outline they owe much to Greene's romantic heroines — Dorothea, Ida, and Margaret — and to Lyly's witty and fanciful ones. They owe much too in artistic method. The personality lies in the quality and combination of traits and sentiments and the turn of the poetical speech rather than in the ideas or a clearly defined point of view. Shakespeare's maidens in love, like most of his other characters, are the consummation and perfection of types established on the stage. Like all great popular art, his is nobly traditional. In his figures you recognize the lineaments of the ' primitives ' as you do in the Madonnas and Saints of Raphael and Leonardo. And consummating, both in substance and in method, the work of their predecessors, Shakespeare and the painters alike satisfied the expectations of their public. To one who, like Chateaubriand, does not belong to the public in question, that effect is less apparent; but in the greatest art, which aims at arousing the emotions, it is indispensable.

10

I would say something of the maidens' lovers, for they are fitting mates, if not for life (as George Eliot or Henry James would have them) — if not clearly by tastes or opinions, yet by temperament, certainly, and for conversation and the play. They are perfect partners in the exhilarating fandango or fox-trot of talk. Orlando, for instance, is suited to Rosalind, but not to Beatrice, with whom he could scarcely keep up in repartee. In this matter, however, Shakespeare is, again, old-fashioned; love is enough, and companionship; while he generally exhibits an affinity of temperament he does not demonstrate it, and for a community of ideas and principles, social or political, æsthetic or religious, shows no concern.

I would say something, too, of other maidens of

Shakespeare's prime — Hero and Celia, Helena and Cressida, Princess Katharine and even Anne Page. Indeed, I will now endeavour to do so, sometimes illustrating the point upon which I have already touched — that in Shakespeare's art the traits are striking and attractive apart from or despite the connexion, as not in the classic art of Racine.

There is Hero, the sweetest lady that Claudio ever looked on, who, on Don Pedro's proposal to fool Benedick and Beatrice into falling in love with each other, declares, thus showing herself worthy of Beatrice's later demonstration of loyalty, that she will do any modest office to help her cousin to a good husband. Most of Jane Austen's good young ladies might in substance have said the same; such, more frankly then than now, was the aim of feminine friendship. But Hero's sweetness and gentleness are exquisitely in keeping not only with her ordinary demeanour but with her simple dignity when she is insulted in the church.

There is Celia, who, though she too plays a secondary role, but with no such tragic experience, is interesting enough to be for Rosalind what Hero is probably not for Beatrice, an adequate companion in life. As of her own accord she follows her cousin into exile, she says of Touchstone,

> He'll go along o'er the wide world with me,

which indeed he seems quite ready to do. And she is also imaginatively sympathetic enough to be Rosalind's fitting companion on the stage. Without love affairs of her own, she is almost as merry and lively as her love-stricken cousin, and sometimes more so:

> Why, cousin! why, Rosalind! Cupid have mercy, not a word!

and again, when Rosalind vows she will weep:

> Do, I prithee; but yet, have the grace to consider that tears do not become a man.

So she enters into the unreal-real wooing as spiritedly and happily as if the game were hers. 'And I am your Rosalind,' the gaily veracious young lady declares in the guise of Ganymede to Orlando. 'It pleases him to call you so,' breaks in Celia, complimenting even as she catches her up; 'but he hath a Rosalind of a better leer than you.' Many a woman would not have taken so sweetly to her second fiddle, whether in life or on the stage. How Beatrice would have sighed if expected to do it!

And Helena, incredible, ineffable Helena, who did a braver thing than all the worthies did though to win the love of no better a man than Bertram! Here is the chief warrant for Mr. Shaw's notion that women 'hunt the men down,' yet how insufficient! Here is a plain case of Shakespeare's poetry in the treatment of character; this side those realms of gold Helena, in her purity and delicacy and unfaltering devotion, beggars belief. She does not fit into society as we know it, and still less into the Elizabethan. Certain medieval conventions in story are to be allowed for; but only where speech is song and the real gives place to the ideal, would it be possible for such a young woman as she to ask such a young man as Bertram for a parting kiss. Charity seeketh not her own, but it is of another love that the Apostle is there speaking; and this, too, beareth all things, believeth all things, hopeth all things, endureth all things, confident of its power.

And Cressida, — 'maiden' in her case is but a courtesy-title — Cressida, an exception in Shakespeare, a perfect (therefore a charming) coquette and light o' love, languorous and in love with love as Shakespeare's true women are not, but who plays the game for all she is worth, trolls the tongue and rolls the eye, invites Troilus and in the same breath denies him, murmurs the honeyed syllables of her yearning and yet bids him 'stop my mouth,' whimpers, when he hears the call of duty,

> Are you a-weary of me?

and would entice and beguile him with her amorous pouting, her pleadings and reproaches:

> Príthee, tárry.
> You mén will néver tárry.
> O foólish Créssid! I might have still héld óff,
> And thén you woúld have tárried.

'You men!' — for well she knows what they are like, and by what means she has kept them, and that to any other of them she would here be betraying herself, but not to this big open-hearted boy.

And Princess Katharine of France, who though a coquette is a proper and innocent one, a coquette born — as according to English notions French young women all are — and who, when King Henry demands of her whether she can love him, replies that she cannot tell, that it shall be as pleases ' le roi mon père,' and avers that Henry has false French enough to deceive the most sage demoiselle that is in France.

And sweet but sensible Anne Page, in a fairly real and workaday Windsor, who, in Slender's prettily appropriate though inadequate words, ' has brown hair and speaks small, like a woman,' but who has a mind not to throw herself away on a Slender, nor, indeed, though she takes to him, on a Fenton, either, and when he complains that her father thinks he is after her for her property, coolly but archly answers him, ' May be he tells you true.' There, for once in Shakespeare, love speaks the tongue not of romance but of this everyday world, for Anne is not high-born as Shakespeare's other heroines are; unlike the others, she is not of the *beau monde*, was never in Arcadia; and yet in a moment she too, like a lady, puts on a disguise and elopes! For what young woman in her condition, whether in or out of Shakespeare, believes her father or obeys him?

LECTURE III

The Maidens of the Dramatic Romances

I

IN the heroines of Shakespeare's last period there is a perceptible change. The so-called dramatic romances — *Cymbeline, The Winter's Tale,* and *The Tempest,* with *Pericles* by rights included — resemble the comedies of his early manhood, such as *The Merchant of Venice, Much Ado,* and *As You Like It,* rather than those of his middle period, *All's Well* and *Measure for Measure,* and repeat, though modified, some of the types of character and situation. Both sorts of comedy are romantic and sentimental, poetical and lyrical, and represent, in the same play, high life and low, serious and comic; but now the serious element is preponderant, the romantic quality more extravagant. As in the dramatic romances of Calderón, it is a land of nowhere, a time indeterminate — Bohemia with a seacoast, where people bear classical names, in the day of an Emperor of Russia and of the painter Julio Romano; or a mythical Britain, after the conquest by Julius Caesar; or a desert isle, in a sea unnamed. And the place prepares us for the action, which is like that of a fairy-tale, with magical charms and supernatural appearances, spirits and monsters, exposure of infants and their recovery, shipwrecks and miraculous rescues, apparent deaths and spectacular revivals. From ordinary life we are remote. The mood, accordingly, is dreamy, in the good sense of the word sentimental, and this is reflected by the heroines. Wit is not for them, but humour, and not the high-powered sort, either, of Rosalind or Beatrice. 'The love-making of Rosalind and Orlando,' says Mr. Moorman, 'or of Beatrice and Benedick, is chiefly in prose; that of Perdita and Florizel, or Miranda and Ferdinand, is almost entirely in verse; and, in place of gay repartee and fusillades of wit, Shakespeare introduces into these love-scenes a note of tenderness, a spirit of chivalrous devotion, and an atmosphere of idyllic beauty.'

Idyllic but not dramatic: wit, we have seen, may be a dramatic asset. There is nothing really dramatic in the relations of these young lovers except — for Hermione, as twice a mother, is out of consideration — in those of Imogen; and here is only the external misunderstanding that arises from slander. The idyllic and romantic is carried farther or higher than ever before, and so is the ideal. One quality which we have noticed especially in Viola becomes now more prominent, the love that is self-forgetful and self-denying. It is the glory of Imogen as of Hermione, and, less heroically, of Miranda.

2

Inquiry into the cause for the change I shall postpone to the end of our discussion, and turn immediately to the characters themselves. Imogen, by fairly common consent, is the finest achievement among Shakespeare's virtuous women. ' Range out the great gallery of good women,' says Sir Arthur Quiller-Couch, — 'Silvia, Portia, Beatrice, Rosalind, Viola, Helena, Isabella, Marina, Perdita — Heavens, what a list [but the married ones Sir Arthur is omitting] — and over them all Imogen bears the bell.' Not, of course, that she is better morally, but that she is the most interesting and charming, the most complex and various, the most equal to whatever happens, good or evil. Under the heaviest blows of Fortune she bears up or rebounds. And her resilience and variety are equalled by her delicacy and intensity. Even Mr. Shaw, though he finds much fault with her or he would be untrue to himself (which Mr. Shaw could never be), calls her ' an enchanting person of the most delicate sensitiveness, full of sudden transitions from ecstasies of tenderness to transports of childish rage, and reckless of consequences in both, instantly hurt and instantly appeased, and of the highest breeding and courage.' But the best of it is that a love so ardent is not self-absorbed or all-engrossing. Like Hermione, she imagines excuses for her deluded husband, thinks with a pang of what he will suffer when he shall see the light. What is more remarkable, in grief or joy she has a place in her mind and heart even for those

87

who have no connexion with it. Amid her suffering she has consideration and tenderness for Pisanio, her husband's servant; and amid the delight of recovering her husband she rejoices in the recovery of her long-lost brothers.

The enchantment of her, the very identity of her is, as generally in Shakespeare, realized in her utterance. Her psychology, we shall see, — that is, her mental structure and point of view — is not clearly or consistently indicated. Indeed, it is not motives or *arrières pensées* that are given us but the external psychology — the surface of the mind — temperament and inclinations, sentiments and ways of thinking, as they hang together; and after the Shakespearean fashion, these traits — her charms and virtues, like her freaks and fancies and womanish weaknesses — take on an individual cast and turn of speech, fall into an appropriate and inalienable melody and rhythm, though changing to suit mood and occasion. Even her greater complexity appears in the style and verse — if these are not rather the cause of it. 'Juliet,' Arthur Symons observes, 'has her few notes and no more, her formal tunes; while Imogen can set the whole of Shakespeare's brain to a music as various and uncapturable as the wind.' That is to say, she is of so subtle and elusive a substance because the poet now has at command a medium that can lend such a conception a being.

At its best this various and uncapturable music is heard in the scene where Imogen gets word from her husband to meet him at Milford Haven, which, Mr.

Shaw declares, 'might have been written for Miss Terry, so perfectly does its innocent and frank gladness fit into her hand.' At sight of the treacherous letter she is at once on tiptoe of expectation; she thinks of everything but what we think. Her whole nature has by love been awakened; every part of it is now given play, and vibrates in the verse:

Who? Thy Lord? That is, my lord, Leonatus!
O, learn'd indeed were the astronomer
That knew the stars as I his characters;
He'd lay the future open. You good gods,
Let what is here contain'd relish of love,
Of my lord's health, of his content, — yet not
That we two are asunder; let that grieve him:
Some griefs are medicinable [wholesome]: that is one of
    them,
For it doth physic love . . .

The range of her flight is as far as the thought of that one thing in the world for which she would not have Posthumus happy; and the flutter of humour in her tenderness gives life to the rhythm:

                                  yet nót
  That wé twó are asúnder; let thàt griéve him;
  Some griéfs are médicinable: thát is one of them,
  For it doth phýsic lóve.

To her way of thinking the *remedium amoris* is only a deeper draught, not a taste but the whole brimming cup. And in

                Yóu goòd góds
  Lét what is here contaín'd rélish of lóve,

how her heart trembles and opens wide to receive it!
Still higher rises her excitement after the reading:

O for a horse with wings! Hear'st thou, Pisanio?
He is at Milford-Haven. Read, and tell me
How far 'tis thither. If one of mean affairs
May plod it in a week, why may not *I*
Glide thither in a day? Then, true Pisanio, —
Who long'st, like me, to see thy lord; who long'st, —
But in a fainter kind; — O, not like me,
For mine's beyond beyond — say, and speak thick, —
Love's counsellor should fill the bores of hearing,
To the smothering of the sense — how far it is
To this same blessed Milford; and by the way
Tell me how Wales was made so happy as
To inherit such a haven; but first of all
How we may steal from hence, and for the gap
That we shall make in time, from our hence-going
And our return, to excuse. But first how get hence . . .

Her thought has wings, and her words, to keep up with it; and these love-born fancies, of gliding a week's journey in a day, of Milford itself as blessed, and of Wales as happy to inherit such a haven — to be touched by her lord's feet — are, though now heightened, wholly in keeping with her 'mental habit' in general. Either from fancy to fancy she is carried or to the uttermost limits of one. Near the beginning of the play, after Posthumus' departure, she reproaches Pisanio for not standing on the quay and watching him out of sight:

I would have broke mine eye-strings, crack'd them, but
To look upon him, till the diminution

Of space had pointed him sharp as my needle;
Nay, follow'd him, till he had melted from
The smallness of a gnat to air, and then
Have turn'd mine eye and wept.

(What a darting lightness in the verse for the flight, what slack and pathetic regularity for the relapse!) And thereupon she repines, because, her leave-taking interrupted, she has not been able to make certain business-like arrangements and engagements with him, in light superiority to space and time:

>   charg'd him
> At the sixth hour of morn, at noon, at midnight
> To encounter me with orisons, for then
> I am in heaven for him.

They are like other youthful pairs, of different sex or the same, who on parting vow to each other ever to remember and look together at the sun as he sets and the moon as she rises, without allowance for longitude.

And when, to resume, the fateful news is out, Imogen, though now stricken, is not crushed. In a moment she defends herself, not, like Desdemona, drooping as she does it, but spiritedly, and even with humour as well as tenderness. It is the same voice, in different mood and key. There is still something of the pulsing rhythm; the wings that took the air still flutter and quiver, though on the ground:

False to his bed? What! is it to be false
To lie in watch there and to think on him;

To weep 'twixt clock and clock; if sleep charge nature,
To break it with a fearful dream of him
And cry myself awake? That's false to's bed, is it?

What trepidation in

To bréak it with a feárful dréam of him!

And the humour appears as she carries out her figure, pathetically, to its limits:

Poor I am stale, a garment out of fashion;
And for I am richer than to hang by the walls,
I must be ripped — *To pieces with me!* —

Do thy master's bidding, kill me. When thou see'st him,
A little witness my obedience.

So it appears as, laying bare her heart, she comes upon his love-letters:

What is here?
The scriptures of the loyal Leonatus,
All turn'd to heresy?

and as Pisanio declares that since he received the command he has not slept one wink:

Do't, *and to bed then.*

Was ever any one so gallant and game when heart-broken? Early in the action she cries out to the Queen upon her booby son, aspirant for Imogen's hand, who has undertaken to attack his rival:

> To draw upon an exile! O brave sir!
> I would they were in Afric both together,
> Myself by with a needle, that I might prick
> The goer-back.

For of her lover she expects as much as of herself; and thus, even in her anger, she follows her thought out to the end.

She is a pretty fighter; but that is on the surface, and in her story love is ' the beginning and the end of all.' At the outset she gives her betrothed a ring:

> This diamond was my mother's. Take it, heart;
> But keep it till you woo another wife,
> When Imogen is dead.

In the last scene, when the trouble has been cleared away, she exclaims, as she embraces him, looking into his eyes in complete surrender:

> Why did you throw your wedded lady from you?
> Think that you are upon a lock [wrestling grip] and now
> Throw me again.

This speech is the right musical response to the other, but with a passion and a humour that experience has accumulated and the situation has exalted. It is the rest-tone to the song of her story, and it is harmoniously appropriate in the play that she should say no more; but the fulness and roundness of her nature would not be apparent if it were not that the King, her father, now notices, benignly, how

Posthumus anchors upon Imogen,
And she, like harmless lightning, throws her eye
On him, her brothers, me, her master [Lucius], hitting
Each object with a joy.

Even in the midst of her greatest happiness or sorrow she has remembered the servant as a person, with virtues and feelings of his own — 'good Pisanio,' 'true Pisanio,' 'good fellow,' 'Thou art all the comfort the gods will diet me with' — which lovers seldom do. It is in *their* ego-centric vein to think, if not always to cry out, like Cleopatra when any other specimen of the sex appears,

How much unlike art thou Mark Antony!

But Imogen's eye now lightens upon them all.

3

Her psychology, I said, has caused trouble. She for a moment believes the ill that Iachimo speaks of her husband as early in the play he attempts to seduce her; though unwillingly, she is led by her husband's friend to believe the tale of his libertinism in Italy. But as I have elsewhere [1] undertaken to show, Imogen believes Iachimo only as Othello did Iago, to the point of disbelieving his friend and his wife; and as Gloster did Edmund, to the point of disbelieving his good son, Edgar; and again, more exactly, as Macduff did Malcolm, both when he slandered himself and afterwards

1 *Art and Artifice in Shakespeare* (1933), pp. 36–7.

when he contradicted the slander; and even as Posthumus is presently to believe Iachimo in the account he renders: — all alike without any internal reason for doing so. It is a convention such as underlies the story of Potiphar's wife, of Phaedra and Hippolytus, of Sthenoboea and Bellerophon; people in old story — and this one is Boccaccio's — accept, without any natural inclination or psychological predisposition, what they are untruly but cunningly told. In hearkening they are not to be held credulous or suspicious; the inclination, though it would improve the psychology, would spoil the story. It is a device which expeditiously brings about a complication, a situation dramatically rich and fruitful, with contrasts and ironies; and by psychology this, like the later more momentous situation between Iachimo and Posthumus, is confused or distorted. Thus Imogen becomes, as by a great living critic has even been asserted — and from that there is no escape! — ' a bit of a fool'; the dexterous and clever Iachimo becomes ' crassly blundering '; and Posthumus, crediting Iachimo's report, must be supposed a ' man out of his senses,' harbouring a ' shadow of a doubt ' in his bosom from the outset. Thus hero and heroine, both, lose much of their romantic glory, and still more of our sympathy; while Imogen is thereupon doubly a fool as, in the latter part of the scene, after accepting Iachimo's disavowal and amends, she forgives him to the point, despite her recent experience with him, of taking charge of his trunk for safe-keeping in her bedroom.

Really, the improbabilities in her conduct and that of Iachimo and Posthumus hang together, and superficially, but adequately for Shakespeare's dramatic purposes, justify one another. Why shouldn't Imogen believe Iachimo if her husband can make such a wager and for such a trial give him a letter of introduction? If she can believe a man slandering her husband whom an hour before she had never seen, why shouldn't she believe him when he declares that it was only an *essai de vertu* and praises him again? If then she can believe him anew, why shouldn't she frankly and trustfully take charge of his treasure? And if Posthumus has consented beforehand to let belief in his wife and winning of the wager hinge upon the evidence of conquest which the challenger shall bring back with him, what more can he ask than the bracelet in the seducer's hand and the description of her chamber and her person upon his lips? But if psychological considerations are heeded, Imogen becomes steadily more gullible, Iachimo more preposterous, and Posthumus more gullible and suspicious both.

That, without damaging the play, manifestly cannot be; for we are intended and warmly invited to think well of Imogen and even of Posthumus. One suspicious by nature needs somewhat more than remorse and forgiveness at the end to restore him to our esteem; and a bit of a fool is sadly incompatible with a romantic heroine or hero either, at any rate in Elizabethan days. Even what danger is involved in the convention Shakespeare, so far as Imogen is concerned, is careful to avoid. She believes Iachimo with difficulty, only for a moment; and once he makes clear to her the nature of his proposal for revenge, which she is innocently slow to grasp, she breaks out in all her native character —

What, ho, Pisanio! —

and is straightway for putting him out of the house. Moreover, her readiness to believe Iachimo in his disavowal and amends and to keep the trunk in her chamber is, if taken superficially and not psychologically, to her credit. It heightens the impression of her generosity and proves her disposition to think the best of and do the most for her husband's friend. Suspiciousness, even with reason for it, is not attractive: frankness and open-heartedness, without reason for them, are. When, on the other hand, she learns of Posthumus' bloody instructions to his servant, her notion that it is owing to some evil woman's influence upon him is, by Elizabethan standards at least, an excuse for him and likewise to her credit. That is one of her ideas which cause Mr. Shaw, he boldly and drolly confesses, to 'wince.' (Both in years and in spirit Mr. Shaw is a Victorian, in spite of himself.) Imogen is only like most good and affectionate women, even in our time, in preferring to think that her lover has fallen into the clutches of a vampire rather than that he has voluntarily abandoned her and formed against her evil designs unaided. Just so, good parents will have it that their wicked son has been led astray. *Their* taste, unlike that of the critics, is not, in such a matter at least, for a character wholly in keeping with his conduct. Or if, as Francis Thompson takes it, ' this glorious Imogen' is here bursting ' into a fit of thoroughly feminine but altogether charming jealousy,' it is also a very momentary one. In any case he in the main is right; and like Shakespeare's other women, Desdemona, for instance, who once lies to her husband, she is no insipidly patient or faultless Griselda.

Not in the psychology does the trouble lie, for strictly speaking, there is none, but only character-drawing; not there, but in what may be called the sentiments and ethics, or rather the poetical structure of the play. It is not Imogen's or Posthumus' credulity that spoils the effect but the consequences — the hero's treacherous and murderous undertaking against her and her forgiveness and acceptance of him. The credulity is relieved or supported by one convention: the forgiveness and acceptance are produced by another, to us still less acceptable, that of the cheerful ending for comedy. In Shakespeare the cheerful ending is marriage; and in *Cymbeline* there is the same arbitrary reconciliation as afterwards in *The Winter's Tale*, and before this in *The Two Gentlemen of Verona, As You Like it, Much Ado, All's Well* and *Measure for Measure*. This is, we must admit, an unhappy result of the superficial, merely narrative motivation, which, like the other Elizabethans, Shakespeare practises generally, in comedy and tragedy alike. It is all very well for his heroes and heroines to fall in love, as in the first lecture we saw them do, without much knowledge of each other's character; it is another matter when the heroines eagerly marry or take their husbands back in full possession of such knowledge and despite it. Imogen, Celia, Julia, Hero, Helena, and Mariana, accept their partners for life with almost as little consideration of past experience as for a minuet. And the last two named even go out of their way to get them, taking the place, for the night, of other women. It is pleaded that these matters were in the source; but why, as Mr. Kellett says,[2] did Shakespeare choose such sources? and Mariana's substitution, approved by the Duke and the saintly Isabella, was the dramatist's own addition. It is pleaded that the medieval narrative interest in woman's virtue and in her cleverness, to the point of making them override all limits, and the belief in the indissolubleness of matrimony and a woman's marital rights,[3] still prevailed; for Helena is married to Bertram and Mariana contracted to Angelo. But what of the other women, whose future well-being is so lightly regarded by both the dramatist and themselves? On the whole it cannot be denied that Shakespeare has presented no elevated conception of marriage — in comedy, when a situation is at stake. From *Love's Labour's Lost* to *The Winter's Tale* he or his audience or both together suffer from an insatiable craving to see every Jack have his Jill, without the justification of Molière. Shakespeare's comedies generally are not comedies as Molière's are, but tragicomedies; and too much must be forgiven or con-

[2] *Suggestions* (1923), chapter vi, 'Shakespeare and Marriage.'
[3] Cf. W. W. Lawrence, *Shakespeare's Problem Comedies* (1931).

trived, before the end. The fundamental justification, and not a perfect one, is something like Mr. Murry's, which applies also to Shakespeare's tragedy, and indeed is offered not in connexion with this ingenious or arbitrary pairing of people off but in answer to strictures upon the tuft-hunting of Bassanio and the unfilial conduct of Jessica:

> One cannot too often emphasize the nature of Shakespeare's dramatic 'method.' It was not chosen by him, neither was it imposed upon his reluctant genius; it was simply the condition of the work he had chosen to do . . . The method of Shakespeare's drama consists, essentially, in the humanization of melodrama.[4]

This humanization was mainly by way of the consistency and the charm of trait and speech, and the admiration of the other characters, both of which together are not enough to establish the deeper-seated consistency and identity that as readers, if as play-goers not so much, we nowadays demand or take for granted. ' A few — years ago,' sighs or sobs Paula Tanqueray shortly before she kills herself. ' O God! A few years ago! ' A woman of that sort at three, cries Mr. Shaw, is already the same as at thirty-three. But with Proteus and Angelo and Oliver it is not a matter of years but days or hours, not before the play began, either, but in our very presence; and gladly we here fall back upon trait and speech.

4 *Shakespeare* (N. Y., Harcourt, Brace & Co., 1936) pp. 163-4.

4

On Perdita and Miranda we cannot dwell long. The one is more flexible and various, more blooming and irresistibly engaging; the other, more ignorant, innocent, ethereal. The one finds nature and life about her more interesting; the other knows little of either and to her the isle really is a ' desert.' The one has a sense of humour; the other is among conditions and surroundings that have provoked and require none. The one is less self-forgetful and self-denying — that quality in the play is represented by Hermione, her mother; the other is lost in devotion to her father and then to her lover when he appears.

Neither maiden, however, arouses a really dramatic interest; and Perdita is almost limited to a scene. Shakespeare's constructive power is growing uncertain. The descriptive is getting the upper hand of the dramatic; the idyllic, of the realistic; character, of the action; charming detail, of the structure as a whole. But with the result who would quarrel, ' that infinitely gracious picture of the Shepherd's feast,' to quote Mr. Moorman, ' at which Perdita, a radiant queen of curds and cream, presides as hostess of the meeting and scatters her largesse of flowers upon old and young? ' Of the flower poetry I cannot permit myself to speak except to call your attention to the fact that the life-giving, anthropomorphic tendency of Shakespeare's Elizabethan imagination, as we find it, for instance, in *A Midsummer*

Night's Dream, has now taken a new and more delicate turn.
> The cowslips tall her pensioners be,
> In their gold coats spots you see,

and that is a pretty and quite plausible fancy; the cowslips — English, not American or Canadian, of course — really are like Queen Elizabeth's pensioners in their gay garments and bonnets. But in the

> daffodils,
> That come before the swallow dares, and take
> The winds of March with beauty,

there is not comparison but only suggestion, and not of the looks but (so to speak) of the spirit: there is not the imitative or pictorial quality but the essentially, exclusively poetical, and the yellow flower flaunting in the winds is a little minx or hussy who has ventured foremost into the sunshine to captivate them and revel in their caresses. How characteristic the fancy is of Perdita, innocently familiar with the ways of 'great creating nature,' sprightly and humorous, exquisite and tender! She is nearer the earth than Miranda and has more facets to her character; she has more of both the knowledge and the joy of life in her, and her song is full of trills and grace notes, of starts and sallies of girlish charm. More buoyant and resilient, she is given to exclamations and apostrophes. 'I bless the time,' cries Florizel,

> When my good falcon made her flight across
> Thy father's ground.

'Now Jove afford thee cause,' she chimes in. 'Lift up your countenance,' he bids her, as she is fearful of meeting his father:

>>as it were the day
>>Of celebration of that nuptial which
>>We two have sworn shall come.

'O lady Fortune, stand you auspicious,' she happily, tremulously implores. And her speech beginning with 'O Proserpina, for the flowers now that frighted thou let'st fall from Dis's wagon' is the supreme example. She has, moreover, a pretty and feminine petulance about her. When Polixenes argues that the products of the gardener's art are not unnatural or illegitimate, to the point of convincing her, and thereupon bids her make her garden rich in gillyflowers, she, true woman, is of her own opinion still:

>>I'll not put
>>The dibble in earth to set one slip of them.

What a toss of the head and shake of the curls in the verse! And when Polixenes, at last unmasking himself, breaks up the match, there is in her words to Florizel 'that profound nature of noble pride and grief, venting themselves in a momentary peevishness of resentment,' admired by Coleridge.

>>Will't please you, sir, be gone?
>>I told you what would come of this: beseech you,
>>Of your own state take care: this dream of mine —
>>Being now awake, I'll queen it no inch farther,
>>But milk my ewes and weep.

Begone! *Va-t-en*, cries Chimène, in a more serious complication, both well knowing that their words will not be heeded.

5

Miranda comes nearer than any other of the women we have considered to the conception of Pope, which he meant for satire but which, despite him, romantic Coleridge, Hazlitt, and De Quincey took for praise:

Most women have no characters at all.

'Every one wishes a Desdemona or Ophelia for a wife,' declares Coleridge, whose own had bidden him 'Get oop' when he knelt, in his mistaken adoration, before her; 'creatures, who, though they may not always understand you, do always feel you, and feel with you.' Desdemona and Ophelia both are created to meet the exigencies of a tragic story; but to the poet the type is dear, though ordinarily placed in secondary roles, as in the case of Hero and Celia. And in Miranda is the culmination of Shakespeare's method of characterization with his maidens by speech and by way of their dependence on the men. She is but a voice, and love is really the sum of her existence. She exists in her relation to others, and takes her colour, positively or negatively, from her surroundings. She has none of Perdita's knowledge or self-assertiveness, her buoyancy and humour, her girlish fancies and caprices: she has only the transparent and receptive emotions of love and wonder. When she hears of her father's sufferings in the past she bethinks her that she was part of them:

> O, my heart bleeds
> To think o' the teen that I have turn'd you to;

and again:

> Alack, what trouble
> Was I then to you!

And when she hears of old Gonzalo, who in this distress was true and loyal, she is gratitude itself:

> Would I might
> But ever see that man!

There we hear her slow sweet accents, look into her wide open eyes! Hers are pellucid pools; Perdita's, sparkling springs. Fortunately 'that man' is not the first Miranda sees, for with the first she straightway falls in love. Her heart too is wide open. At the outset she takes Ferdinand for a spirit: though her father's enemies are approaching, this cannot be one of them. But at once she is his. It is as in the Garden of Eden, and her only practical thought is of her beloved's present sufferings and of relieving them. When Prospero plays the tyrant over him as an enemy, she would be 'his surety'; and not accepted for that, she would carry the logs in his place. Between her and the object of her affection there are no veils or barriers; had she Perdita's knowledge such liberty would not be becoming. She has no inhibitions, as we say, but has need of none. There is nothing of the gipsy or sprite about her. She is no mere child of nature but the daughter of a philosopher, less of a wood-nymph than an angel. She disobeys her father in telling Ferdinand her name, but she does so before she thinks, under a new dispensation. It is she that asks the question 'Do you love me?' though in a manner he has already declared himself —

>   for your sake
> Am I this patient log-man;

and his answer being in the affirmative, all is now over. 'My husband, then.' And that, thus early in the play, is the end of Miranda's story; as it was of most good women's in both Pope's and Coleridge's time, and practically is in Shakespeare's other comedies.

At the beginning of the lecture I said that in these later plays romance is carried farther and higher than ever before, to the detriment of drama; and in *The Tempest*, presumably Shakespeare's last unaided work, it reaches the limit or pinnacle. When two souls are wholly pure and simple, all barriers (as between Coleridge's Genevieve and her lover) either lacking or burned away — when there is no longer pretence or deception, nor even, as ordinarily in Shakespeare, a disguise or a play of wits — then, as here in *The Tempest*, there is little place left for drama. Extremes, as in the first lecture we noticed, often meet, high romantic spirits surrender to each other (though with what a difference!) as simply and completely as the silly and the irresponsible — and then, as Shakespeare seems to have recognized, the dramatist's occupation's gone.

6

Students have wondered why these later women are so much more idyllic and Arcadian than the earlier, closer to Nature and the flowers, more serious and ethereal, more self-forgetful and self-denying, and bathed in the light less of earth than of heaven. And of course they have answered.

One explanation, which is easy, is that Shakespeare himself was now at Stratford, actually among the flowers and nearer to Nature unspoiled. Another is that we have here the influence of Beaumont and Fletcher in their romances, as in *Philaster* and the *Maid's Tragedy*, where there are maidens somewhat like these; and the influence of the Court taste for masques, Prince Henry himself, the bright luminary of St. James's, appearing in Florizel and Ferdinand on the stage. Still another, Professor J. D. Wilson's, is that Shakespeare at the time of the great tragedies had undergone a great spiritual crisis and a physical collapse, and now at Stratford had, in family life and in the country, which God made (as not the town), found healing for his soul. He was 'near to madness' when he wrote *King Lear*, and 'in the terrible and unfinished' *Timon* there is ' evidence of a complete breakdown.' Shakespeare is another Wordsworth — are there two great English poets much more different? — and as

Wordsworth's spirit was restored by Westmorland and his sister, so was Shakespeare's by Warwickshire and his daughter; as the Romantic poet recovered by falling in love a second time with the Lake Country, so the dramatist and actor recovered by falling a second time in love with Stratford, or the country round about. This last interpretation, of course, hangs together with the notion that the desert isle in *The Tempest* is Life itself, or the world; that Milan is Stratford, and Prospero Shakespeare, the prodigious magician, or, as Sir Edmund Chambers calls him, the 'Duke of Stratford'; that Ariel is his genius, and Miranda the drama; and that Caliban is the vulgar public, or any of the other strange things he has been taken to be.

There was a time when English literature was not considered a fit subject of university instruction; that was when psychology and sociology and subjects still vaguer and more variable were not either, and I sometimes suspect that the study of English literature was the entering wedge and the beginning of our present academic degeneration and decay. Not that psychology or sociology, in their nobler and more solid manifestations, are at all valueless; but these studies, prone to conspire together, pass themselves off for history, and thereupon the trouble begins. Could explanation be more irrelevant or illogical than this that I have just repeated, or in the effort to be historical, less so? What would Shakespeare himself or any other clear-headed person before the day of Wordsworth's transcendental nature-worship have thought of a man's recovering from a physical or spiritual malady by falling in love with Stratford or Warwickshire or any other region of the earth, or, indeed, how would the man himself have gone about it? What would the bard of Avon — or Spenser, Jonson, or Milton, for that matter — have made of the *Sonnets to the River Duddon,* the *Cuckoo* or the *Celandine,* or of the more mystical passages in the *Prelude* or the *Excursion?* Provided, of course, in the first place, that a malady or break-down, spiritual or physical, there really was. Of that what does any of us know, or of Shakespeare's relations to his daughter, or, at the time of writing these plays, even of his place of residence? To me it is all mere conjecture, arising (like the assumption that Florizel or Ferdinand must be a living celebrity whom Shakespeare knew of, or the correlative assumption that young Prince Henry as the most popular young notable of his day must be somewhere reflected in Shakespeare's drama) out of the preconception that, poetry being the imitation of life, bits of the contemporary life can there be identified, or that the objects described, such as flowers and maidens, must be in the immediate neighbourhood. If the mirror is held up to nature, why, then, everything must be visible in it, though in a Bohemia-Warwickshire Prince Henry can have no very pressing claims. Flowers there were, and innocent maidens, too, round about Stratford then as there are today; but even we, who are not poets, are likely, in our brooding, poetical moments, to think of the country when in the city, and of our native land when in foreign parts, like Wordsworth himself in Germany! The implication — that poetry is a transcript, is history, or autobiography, which I have dwelt on elsewhere — I cannot now reconsider. But these critics forget the nature of poetry, the rights, privileges, and immunities of the imagination, and even the explicit words of that priest of Nature (also one of the greatest of critics) whom they invoke. To the poet Wordsworth ascribes 'a disposition to be affected more than other men *by absent things as if they were present;* an ability of conjuring up in himself passions, which are indeed far from being the same as those produced by real events yet . . . do more nearly resemble the passions produced by real events than anything which, from the motions of their own minds merely, other men are accustomed to feel in themselves; — whence, and from practice, he has acquired a greater readiness and power in expressing what he thinks and feels, and especially those thoughts and feelings which, by his own choice, or from the structure of his own mind, arise in him without immediate external excitement.' Such is or is supposed to be the poet's prerogative, his native and inalienable advantage. Mr. Somerset Maugham, of course, is right: 'The imagination can create nothing out of the void, it needs the stimulus of sensation.' Its work is creation, however, not imitation. The emotion is 'remembered in tranquillity,' from a distance; indeed, it is ordinarily not one emotion or experience but many combined, transformed, and, as Mr. Eliot says, concentrated;[5] and by reader or investigator, however ingenious, the stimulus is not easily or certainly to be detected or identified, or it does not turn out to be much of anything when it is. If of late the originals of Justice Shallow and his nephew, Slender, have really been discovered in Southwark, both are, in Shakespeare's text, at all events, very different beings. So it is, as Mr. Maugham himself demonstrates, with his own stories; in his *Before the Party* the only fact is that an Englishman in the East Indies, until cured of the habit by his wife, regularly took a bottle of whiskey to bed with him. Taking the bottle to bed was the stimulus — Mr. Maugham's of course — and that he had only heard of! And if Stratford, the poet's daughter, or Prince Henry really figures in the dramatic romances, they are all made so unrecognizable that the sort of spectator or reader the poet expected is not troubled by the alien presence.

7

Another notion involved is that great poetry must include symbolism: and that when one denies its presence in Shakespeare's, one betrays in oneself a want of poetical or spiritual sense. Just so one is charged with being insensible to character, and, strange to say, blind to ideal values, if one discovers in Shakespeare no psychology that goes beyond character-drawing. The

---

[5] For Mr. Maugham see his Preface to *Altogether;* for Mr. Eliot, *Selected Essays* (N. Y., 1932), pp. 7–10.

critics are unmindful that some of the greatest characters in all literature, like Homer's Achilles and Odysseus, Sophocles' OEdipus and Antigone, are without a psychology (and having no serious fault are therefore only the more ideal); just as the greatest poetry, like nearly all that of the Greeks and Latins, the best of Chaucer, yes and of Dante, too, nearly all of Milton, Wordsworth, and Browning, and of the Elizabethan (like the Bourbon) drama, is wanting in symbolism or allegory. In the same spirit the critics demand a philosophy or a spiritual message of tragedy, and sad work they make of the text before they find it there. Really symbolism has no place on the stage except such as there is in Ibsen's *Ghosts* and the *Master-Builder* (and, for that matter, in Dante and Spenser when it is successful), which needs no critic to discover, to expound and exploit it.

8

Surely it is more reasonable and relevant to explain the nature of Shakespeare's later female characters, not on the basis of the poet's experience, whereof we know nothing, but of his art whereof we should know something; and in the poetic dramatist's natural development lies an explanation already laid bare. As we have seen, he followed his romantic bent. There is a connexion between the poet's 'romances' and those of Beaumont and Fletcher, but whether his or theirs were first in the field will probably never be determined. In *Philaster* and *The Maid's Tragedy* there are three young women — Arethusa, Aspatia, Euphrasia — who have a self-effacingness like that of Imogen, Hermione, and Miranda, and idyllic traits like those of Perdita. But, except for the situation of injured innocence, these last have as much or more in common with Viola; and Shakespeare's later young women are naturally and legitimately akin to the earlier ones. *Twelfth Night,* the 'farewell to mirth,' is supposed immediately to precede the period of the great tragedies: in these the young heroines in love are similarly, but more loftily, self-sacrificing — Ophelia, Desdemona, Cordelia; and when Shakespeare in his final period reverted, like other great artists, to the mood and style of his first, and, somewhat like Ibsen and Goethe, became romantic again, it was only natural that, as with them, qualities of the early period should blend with those which had developed since. Moreover, it is the tendency of an art, whether of the individual practitioner or of the group, to work out to the limit, though after an interval, a *motif* once found fruitful and acceptable; and in a romantic type of drama, in which comedy was subordinated and romance was exaggerated, it was a matter of taking the path of least resistance that the taste of artist and public both should turn again to this type of heroine, now further to be etherealized till it scarcely touches the earth. Imogen, Hermione, and Miranda are the result. Shakespeare's genius and the temper of his public offer a far better explanation of the change in his art than any personal experience, particularly one invented for the purpose of explanation, derived, in fact, from the work of art to be explained.

Above all, too little allowance is made for what Wordsworth himself calls the 'indestructible dominion' of the imagination. In its supreme manifestations it is not dependent upon models, and especially in the artist's later days. When working in the Sistine chapel, Michelangelo often could have had no one posing for him, not because he was on a scaffold but because some of the attitudes depicted are physically impossible. Far from bowing down to Nature, he threw off her sway. Music, to be sure, is a less imitative art; but of Beethoven it has been said that his 'third style arose imperceptibly from his second. His deafness had very little to do with it, for all his epoch-making discoveries in orchestral effect date from the time when he was already far too much inconvenienced to test them in a way which would satisfy any one who depended more upon his ear than upon his imagination.' May it not have been so — must it not have been so? — with Shakespeare, a romantic dramatist who had penned more than thirty plays and had been most of his life an actor? If the flowers and the women of his poetry now were those immediately about him at Stratford one would expect some trace of local colour; but there is less realism in them, as we have seen, than in those of his prime; Perdita's very daffodils are not painted with the eye on the object but from memory, and to make a new creation, forms more real than living flower; and Perdita, Imogen, and Miranda alike have nothing about them that relishes of Stratford or Warwickshire. They have, for the most part, the traits of his earlier heroines, but differently combined. If they are more ethereal and dreamy, that is something that comes not out of town or country either. By this time, if not before, the supreme poet had no need of models, the figure, as he took up the pen, arose before him out of the deep; and to adapt the words of Coleridge as applied to Richardson in contrast to Fielding (and Hazlitt says much the same) ' he drew from his own heart and depicted characters beyond the reach of observation.' Had he not been observing all his life long? And where the poet was when he wrote *The Tempest*, or for that matter any of his other great plays, we shall probably never know, nor need we know. Wherever he was, he was not really there. If he was like most poets we read of, poetry was his magic carpet of escape.

9

As now we look back over the subjects of all three lectures, another but kindred question arises. Did the man ever meet such young women as he depicts, whether at this or at any time, or himself enjoy anything of the ' earthly felicity,' as Mr. Murry calls it, of, say, Orlando or Florizel? All that is known is Anne Hathaway and the Dark Lady of the Sonnets, and the latter through the Sonnets merely. From the former he absented himself, at least for long periods, during the best part of his life, which was spent in London; and in his will he coolly and dryly, with not even a conventional testamentary epithet of affection, left her all the world knows what. She was provided for by law, she may have had an attachment to the particular article of furniture in question; but in the first draft she was left out of the will altogether, and by a later interlineation was given that and no more. The other lady he had no reason even on second thoughts to mention there. Positive evidence is lacking; but there is no indication of any earthly felicity with either, and if their traits reappear in the glorious women whom he puts upon the stage, we are none the wiser. The life of many of us, and the best of it, too, is a dream, and that is true preëminently of a poet. His biography, when it is fairly and honestly written, not extracted and reconstructed from his poems, is generally meagre, and often but an irrelevant commentary upon them. His life — not his biography, a different and often a contrary thing — is in them. Shakespeare has been called the poet laureate of love, but what if all he knew of that was through Anne of Shottery, whom he in public thus treated so coolly, and the Siren of the City, whom he hated almost as much as he loved, and did not honour?

Apparitions, then, these women from Julia to Miranda? But as almost no one else ever was, this poet was wholly and irrecoverably a dramatist. These women of his are not dream women, like Poe's or Shelley's, Byron's or Swinburne's. They are not the outcome of incompetence or 'frustration,' 'suppression' or 'sublimation.' They are alike, as Chateaubriand says, but that is because they are not analysed or put in a psychological situation; and because, as to be popular the greatest art must always do, they owe the type or outline to tradition — to Greene and Lyly and the non-dramatic romances. They are alike, but not, as any one poet's dream women generally are, much the same. Indeed, they are not dreamy at all but real and solid, though with the reality and solidity of a law-abiding but autonomous imagination. Upon the problem the Freudians, the psychoanalysts, have long been working, and every new psychology of genius that arises, until the end of time, will, no doubt, take its turn. But, so far, to no avail — and that restores our faith in the dominion of the imagination. Coleridge has the same point of view as Wordsworth. Even in *Venus and Adonis* he remarks 'as a promise of genius the choice of subjects very remote from the private interests and circumstances of the writer himself.' It is not a sign of the writer's genius that in a novel or a play we can recognize the writer himself, his companions or his contemporaries, his wife or his daughter, as we do in the literary work of our friends. There is something wrong when that is the chief source of our pleasure. It is not a sign of genius, either, that your writer should be at home only when the scene is in Warwickshire, in Dorset or Devon, in Vermont or, God save the mark, Iowa or Minnesota, as so frequently he is today; although it is still less of a sign when, in order to make amends for not having been there, he goes to a particular province or district on purpose to get it up. Shakespeare very probably was never in Italy, Rossetti certainly never was. Personal or regional poetry or prose may be of a very high order, and it may have a local colour or flavour that genius unaided can never give it; but 'personal note' or local colour is not the essential thing — the Greeks had neither the thing nor the name; and what genius, the imagination, gives is of higher importance. It can give so much because it has received much, both from the actual world and (as we have noted) from tradition; but all this it changes. A transforming, vitalizing power is what the supreme poet gives, he himself, whether Homer or Shakespeare, remaining, as Hazlitt said of the latter, 'the least of an egotist that it was possible to be.' And if that is a quality of the supreme poet or dramatist, how much the more it may be expected of the poet laureate of love! If in art as in life self-forgetfulness is a virtue, how much more it should be with a subject like this! Of extremes meeting there is no more conspicuous example than in this matter of the impersonal. There is the objectivity which ignores or suppresses the writer's own earthly felicity or infelicity, and there is that which has risen above it. Anne and the Siren, the little happiness and the manifold sorrow they caused him, were only a point of departure for the poet in his flight. And who could attain to so high and wide a notion of love and happiness as he who had a lifelong craving for the one and but a fragment and pitiful taste of the other?